Partnership

and the Benefits of Learning

A Symposium

on

Philosophical Issues in Educational Policy

Edited by Pádraig Hogan

Educational Studies Association of Ireland
Cumann Léann Oideachais na hÉireann

Copyright: The Authors

First published 1995

Educational Studies Association of Ireland.
Maynooth College, Co. Kildare, Ireland.

All rights reserved. Except for the quotation of short passages for the purposes of criticism and review, no part of this publication may be reproduced, stored in a retrieval system, or transmitted, in any form or by any means, electronic, mechanical, photocopying or otherwise, without prior permission of the copyright holders.

This book is sold subject to the condition that it shall not, by way of trade or otherwise, be lent, re-sold, hired out, or otherwise circulated, without the publisher's prior consent in any form of binding or cover other than that in which it is published and without a similar condition being applied to the subsequent purchaser.

ISBN 0 9524696 1 8

CONTENTS

Acknowledgements.. ii

Preface — *Niamh Bhreathnach, T.D., Minister for Education* iii

Pádraig Hogan
Introduction : Educational Policy in Philosophical Perspective   1

Barney O'Reilly
Economics, Politics and The Philosophy of Education in
Ireland.. 12

Eoin Cassidy
Irish Educational Policy : The Place of Religion in a Pluralist
Society.. 29

Questions and Discussion — Session One
Chaired by Áine Hyland.. 52

Joseph Dunne
What's the Good of Education...................................... 60

Kevin Williams
Philosophy and Curriculum Policy................................. 83

Pádraig Hogan
Power, Partiality and The Purposes of Learning................ 107

Questions and Discussion — Session Two
Chaired by Peter McKenna... 121

Notes on Papers... 138

A Note on the Speakers.. 166

ACKNOWLEDGEMENTS

The Educational Studies Association of Ireland is grateful to Dublin City University for agreeing to host this symposium and for assistance in planning it. Special thanks are due to Dr. Peter McKenna, Head of the Faculty of Educational Studies at DCU, who organised the theatre and recording facilities for the symposium, who warmly welcomed the participants and who also arranged to make the university's social facilities available to the participants. Thanks are also due to four students from the Mater Dei Institute of Education, Dublin — Giovana Salvati, Erica Sheehan, Helen Walsh and Ephrem Feeley — who volunteered to handle the registration of the symposium participants. As Editor, I am grateful, firstly, to the Minister for Education, Niamh Bhreathnach, T.D., for contributing the Preface to the book. I am also grateful to my fellow contributors to this volume for wasting no time in preparing the final versions of their papers, to take account of points made in the formal and informal discussions during the symposium. A special word of thanks is due to Monica Dowdall, who prepared the text for printing and whose expertise on matters of layout has been as valuable and unfailing as ever.

PREFACE

Niamh Bhreathnach, T.D., Minister for Education

At the John Marcus O'Sullivan Lecture in March 1993, I asserted that explicit debate on the philosophy underpinning our education system has at best been limited and that we are unlikely to find a well articulated coherent philosophy transparently evident in Irish education. Of its nature, education legislation provides at best an implicit philosophy. Therefore, I concluded that:

> "If we do not achieve a consensual view of a coherent philosophic framework in our debate directed towards framing the White Paper, there is no magic formula which will provide a philosophy when we come to proposing the Bill."

This posed a deliberate challenge to participants in the education debate to join in exploration of this issue. In the intervening twenty months, I have valued contributions from various sources as I have endeavoured to develop and clarify a coherent statement of philosophy against which education policy proposals can be tested and judged.

The symposium on Philosophical Issues in Educational Policy which has given rise to this publication, is a particularly worthwhile and enriching contribution to the debate and, indeed, to the refinement of my own thinking in this area.

I commend the contributors for their admirable clarity of expression which mirrors the clarity of thought evident in their arguments. These arguments leave no room for complacency and certainly achieve, what Dr. Dunne defined as the first task of philosophy: to avoid being consigned to grand statements of aim.

These papers are demanding reading for a Minister. They raise disturbing questions. Do decision makers fail to seek the answer to the pertinent question due to bias, sloth, interest, chance or lack of time? Were pupils the forgotten people, and points the forgotten issue at the Convention? How can we liberate young people in school from the "tyranny of the written word?"

However, the papers not only defy complacency, but also offer vision. They address the essentials of dialogue, the implications of pluralism, the management of schooling and intrinsic good in the context of practice. I could multiply these examples. We are challenged by these papers, but we are inspired rather then depressed. We may disagree with the conclusions but we cannot criticise the energy, vigour and strength of the arguments. The philosopher's role of introducing clarity into discourse, exposing unexamined assumptions, drawing distinctions, detecting fallacious arguments and showing up specious nonsense is pursued by the authors with remarkable force and evident enjoyment.

INTRODUCTION

EDUCATIONAL POLICY IN PHILOSOPHICAL PERSPECTIVE

Pádraig Hogan

Where established custom and routine hold an abiding sway, philosophy is rarely given any task in the public arena other than supplying a justification for existing practices. Such a task tends to give to philosophy the office of apologist, as distinct from that of a questioner of fundamentals, or a self-critical monitor of practice. At its most effective, this apologist conception of philosophy functions as an auxiliary to established authorities in keeping at bay influences which are perceived as hostile. At its worst, it becomes merely a perfunctory or ceremonial feature of public discourse.

Where change establishes itself as a way of life, however, where it displaces traditional conceptions of employment and economic security, where it erodes cultural traditions and religious outlooks of long ancestry, where it swiftly alters the daily patterns of work and leisure, where it canvasses in a particular way the emergent identities of the young, where it progressively succeeds in recasting the economic and social life of an entire society; then philosophy as apologist becomes increasingly irrelevant. In short, it is made redundant by the march of events.

The apologist function of philosophy has become increasingly untenable in the public arena in Ireland since the late sixties. But public recognition of this, particularly by authorities such as church and state, has been slow in coming. The outlooks and practices — for instance, in education, in health care, in social welfare — for which a philosophical apologia was traditionally called upon to do service, have changed dramatically in the last few decades. The extent of this change can be gauged by the extent to which philosophical utterance on matters of public policy has become less clear-cut in its pronouncements, has become more hesitant about its contents as apologia, or has even become ambiguous. Within this ambiguity, however, there still remains an inclination — increasingly a nostalgic one — which seeks to furnish the present with some reassuring picture of loyalties whose secure place was in the past rather than in the present. Fairly recent examples of this kind of public utterance, taken from the field of educational discourse in Ireland, include the following from the Curriculum and Examinations Board (now the National Council for Curriculum and Assessment):—

> The Board acknowledges that a general consensus on the aims of education has long existed in Ireland, and also the general aim of education is to contribute towards the development of all aspects of the individual, including aesthetic, creative, cultural, emotional, intellectual, moral, physical, political, social and spiritual development for personal and family life, for working life, for living in the community and for leisure.[1]

The first of these makes an attempt to call attention to traditions held in common, but it also masks the reality of much that is divisive and parochial in Irish education. The second states that education is to be inclusive in scope rather than preoccupied with just a few aspects of human development. But its blandness, like that of the first statement and of the prose in which they both appear, is a good example of the change that has taken place in philosophical declarations on education in Ireland. We see here a transition from a more assured, and more forthright kind of traditional pronouncement, to a calculated desire to avoid frank and incisive debate on thorny issues; a reluctance to acknowledge real differences and to deal openly with their practical consequences for decision-making in education.

For instance, both statements call attention away from the question of what kinds of "development" would be acceptable or unacceptable, say under the emotional, moral, political, or spiritual "aspects" mentioned in the latter statement. Both call attention away from any identification or appraisal of the kinds of things that might constitute acceptability and unacceptability, under any of the aspects included in the general aim. This bland evasiveness, despite the apparent priority it gives to philosophical aims in education, grants philosophy itself little more than a ceremonial role, and indeed discredits its proper and practical purpose in the public arena. When viewed from a practical perspective, moreover, perhaps it is a belated awareness of this state of affairs, in the face of unprecedented challenges in the daily conduct of education, that has caused philosophical utterance of any kind finally to fall silent in the more recent official publications on education in the Republic. In this connection, the publications of the NCCA, and, in a particular way, the 1992 Green Paper *Education for a Changing World*, are notable examples.[2]

If the demise of philosophy as apologia betokens a situation where little that is traditional and stable now holds an authoritative sway in our society, or in our schools and colleges, then everything becomes newly questionable, if not confusing, and it is here that the more traditional task of philosophy itself is cast once more to the foreground. This task, as exemplified for instance in the career of Socrates, acknowledges generously its debt to tradition, and remains keenly conscious of its responsibilities in the civic community. As a questioning voice in that community however, it realises that the modern body politic — much more so than the competing schools of thought in the Socratic Dialogues — is heir, not just to one major tradition, but to a plurality of traditions which may frequently be in conflict. It also acknowledges that where such plurality is an everyday political reality, and where different interests compete for scarce resources, public discourse is canvassed in many directions, but in approach it is mainly characterised by two contrasting orientations.

The first of these is a custodial, or protectionist orientation — proud of its achievements, keen to advance the rights and privileges of its own case, usually uncritical of its own standpoints, in a democracy tolerant to a greater or lesser degree of other orientations, but generally adversarial towards these wherever they, also, are in the running for limited public resources and legally recognised powers. The second is an orientation towards dialogue, which may be equally proud of particular traditions and achievements, but which views all tradition and all human achievement as being somehow incomplete; as being in continual need of further illumination, and if necessary, of modification. Though this orientation may also be sometimes adversarial towards other standpoints, its character as dialogue ceases if it permits its criticisms here to be more severe or less constructive than any criticism which it is prepared to exercise — or to have exercised by others — on its own standpoints.

Of course, it is rare enough to find either orientation in a pure form wherever public discourse is carried on. Even in the course of a single debate a person's (or a group's) conduct could include elements of both, could even fluctuate between both. It can hardly be denied, however that orientations of a custodial, protectionist and adversarial character are clearly more in evidence in most spheres of human action than are orientations towards dialogue. The most promising office of philosophy in the public arena, nevertheless, is to summon human energies to this latter orientation, and to show that it is an orientation replete with practical possibilities. It is in this spirit that the contributions to this volume seek to respond to the call by the Minister for Education — in the 1993 John Marcus O'Sullivan Memorial Lecture — for a proper philosophical consideration of the major issues in Irish education; issues on which policy decisions for the future must shortly be made.[3]

This was the first call by an Irish Minister for Education for philosophical reflection to enter the public arena in its own right. The Minister's remarks made it clear that what was being called for was an exploration of issues of common concern, openly undertaken by individuals and groups with differing perspectives and traditions. A historical shift of direction was signified by this call, for traditionally, the Department of Education had acquiesced in the conception of philosophical discourse in education which had been embraced by the major interest groups in the field since long before the establishment of the state; namely, the apologist one, where philosophical utterance did service as trusty guardian for standpoints which had already been decided and which were essentially inhospitable to the spirit of questioning and open debate.

And an extensive debate has indeed taken place since the Minister's call in her 1993 lecture and the issuing of the Government's Green Paper the previous year. The publication of the *Report on the National Education Convention* [4] in 1994 marked a key point in that debate, and produced a record of how some significant advances could be achieved through a spirit of genuine dialogue. The Partners in this dialogue were the different participants in the Convention itself and in the Round Table discussions which followed. The *Report on the National Education Convention* called attention however to the need for a further phase in the national debate on education, one which was specifically philosophical. Accordingly, the contributions which follow here have selected some of the more important issues from the education debate and have attempted to bring to them a greater incisiveness, clarity and rigour. The purpose is to seek arguments and policy insights which not only identify enduring benefits of education amid the continual flux of change. Equally important, the search is for arguments and insights which are worthy candidates for *educational commitments as such,* and on grounds which are defensible to a partnership of interests in education rather than on grounds which are those of one interest group as distinct from another.

It has not been possible to include in the symposium all of the major questions which have been raised in the national debate on education up to now. For instance, questions such as the future of higher education and adult education are only marginally touched on in these proceedings. Nor is there a specific presentation on the role of parents, although the concerns and rights of parents are much in evidence in the presentations and discussion sessions. Nevertheless, the issues which are selected for consideration are explored in some depth and many of these are pressed to further clarity in the discussion sessions. In this introduction then, I will try to identify briefly the main themes addressed by each of the five speakers and conclude with a few remarks on how the benefits of learning might best be conceived in a climate where these benefits are continually vulnerable to conquest by the shifting imperatives of change itself.

Eoin Cassidy's presentation, "Irish Educational Policy — The place of religion in a pluralist society" begins by calling attention to the minimalist treatment of religion in *Education for a Changing World.* He contrasts this with the important place given to religion in previous Government documents on education and comments that the change signifies a decisive shift of outlook in policy-making quarters;

a shift which reflects changes in Irish society more generally. He then suggests that the government's education policy now faces the challenge of recognising the importance of religion in Irish culture, particularly in the face of:

(a) the consumerist values of the market;
(b) the rise of a secularist-pluralist society;
(c) the alleged link between denominational education and sectarianism.

He calls attention to disagreements about the truth claims of religion, about its status on the school curriculum, about denominational versus inter-denominational education and about the church's rights to establish and manage its own schools in a pluralist democracy. In reviewing these disagreements, Cassidy argues that Ireland still remains remarkably homogeneous in some key respects, most notably in its continuing allegiance to Christian faith and in its support of the priorities which underpin a market economy.

Recognising the tensions between these two loyalties, Cassidy puts forward a detailed case for religious education in schools and argues that spiritual values have a crucial part to play in the emergent identity of the person; that they offer something invaluable to education in a pluralist society. He is keen, however, to distinguish this educational role from indoctrination. Religious education, in Cassidy's account, brings before us a unique dimension of human life which transcends the material and the secular, and makes a distinctive contribution to education in the best and most inclusive sense of the word. In a postscript to his presentation, Cassidy offers some suggestions on the question of denominational or inter-denominational provision of schooling.

Where Cassidy's presentation to the symposium focuses mainly on the religious dimension of education, Barney O'Reilly's contribution, "Economics, Politics and the Philosophy of Education in Ireland" is concerned mainly with the economic, and with what he calls "the affirmation of ordinary life" (following Charles Taylor). O'Reilly claims that philosophy of education in Ireland has been marked by the absence of a discourse on the economics and politics of education, and that within the philosophy of education itself, there is a failure to engage the questions which arise when economic and

INTRODUCTION 7

political matters come to the fore. He suggests that philosophy of education has been mainly concerned with three main sets of issues:

(a) epistemological issues — exploring the various types of knowledge represented in the curriculum;
(b) intersubjective relations in education — particularly pupil-teacher relations and questions of socialisation; and
(c) theological issues — where questions of church control and school ethos feature prominently.

In each of these areas of philosophical endeavour, O'Reilly discerns a neglect of the concerns of "ordinary life." Such concerns, he points out, include worthy activities such as: schools' contributions to material well-being and the economic productivity of individuals; to the formation of human skills; to the sorting of human resources; to the regulation of labour flows. Some of the other contributors take issue with O'Reilly's claim that philosophy of education in Ireland has neglected economic and political issues.

O'Reilly's presentation traces a parallel between the emergence of economics as a field of study on the one hand, and, on the other, the rise of public schooling, democratic politics and nation states. He is keen that this parallel should be kept in view. He points out that different kinds of schooling have arisen to reflect differences of wealth, social class, ethnic background and religion, and asks whether such differences in provision can be warranted in a democratic society. Among the points he makes towards the end of his presentation is the suggestion that some of the more established forms of communal identity and social organisation have been associated with such distinctions, and are in fact dysfunctional. Yet, he argues, these are often uncritically accepted in the shaping of public policy.

Joseph Dunne's presentation, "What's the Good of Education?" decries the ceremonial function which is all too frequently given to philosophy in policy-making deliberations. He suggests that the bestowal of such an honour often serves to mask the more questionable of philosophical assumptions which remain active among those who engage in this kind of bestowal. In particular, he argues that *Education for a Changing World* violates the integrity of education as a practice by presuming that education itself must be viewed primarily within the context of social and economic change;

that is, as a vehicle which must adapt and re-adapt itself and respond to a host of adventitious demands arising from state, commercial and other interest groups in society. Dunne accepts, however, that an instrumental role for education is essential, not accidental, in any modern society. In this regard he points out that modern education is quite unlike the liberal education of Greek classical civilisation, which was confined to a leisured elite.

Universal schooling has, however, according to Dunne, brought an unwelcome shift in the way that education is conceived in most modern societies, namely as *an investment*. Schools, he points out, cannot afford to ignore the pressures brought by governments, who also provide most of school funds. But the demands of the state can be contradictory: — a socialising function towards democratic convictions and procedures coupled with a social selection function which is antithetical to this, in that it emphasises the promotion of self-interest and private gain. Here Dunne refers to a competitiveness which he calls the most blatant aspect of Irish education, and regrets that it received little attention in the *Report on the National Education Convention.*

Dunne then explores education as a practice, and deals specifically with the benefits of learning. Education as a genuine practice, he argues, has intrinsic goods and standards of excellence. It is through these that personal qualities are nurtured, that desire for inquiry can be awakened and drawn out, that discoveries are made and appreciated, that insights are shared in a way that all can be winners, that limitations can be encountered and accepted, that characteristics like appreciation, receptivity and resourcefulness are acquired, that moral virtues can be practised in an unforced way, that advances can be made in self-esteem and in the uncovering of personal identity. Drawing on examples from traditional practical subjects like woodwork and metalwork, and extending his illustrations to the study of other subjects, Dunne argues that education, as a practice with its own integrity embodies a kind of rationality which makes life more varied, more suggestive and more fulfilling, as distinct from a one-dimensional rationality which deploys a technocratic reasoning almost exclusively — including, he suggests, documents such as the Green Paper — and which creates additional problems for humans.

Kevin Williams begins his contribution, "Philosophy and Curriculum Policy," by voicing some dissatisfaction with the term "philosophy of education" itself. In this he is concerned that the term all too often grants a certain dignity to "high-falutin" utterances and thus allows them to go unchallenged. Williams is a perceptive critic of undetected vacant phrases, particularly where their common currency engenders a comforting but also a counterfeit consensus. He suggests that educational discourse, not least in our own country, is all too burdened with such phrases, and in the opening part of his presentation he gives many examples.

Taking advice from John Locke, Williams argues that philosophy should play the part of an underlabourer rather than any grand role in shaping the course of things. As a detector of unexamined assumptions and inconsistencies, as a guardian of careful argument, he suggests that philosophy can help in determining the persuasiveness of different viewpoints, and can even help to advance a consensus which is something more than mere cliché. He is quick, however, to distinguish the kind if discipline by which such consensus might be advanced from proselytism, and he includes under this latter description the devices and exhortations currently being used, not least in education, to "engineer a new political loyalty" to a "European citizenship."

Where policy decisions are concerned, Williams argues that philosophy can help to concentrate the attentions of policy-makers on where justification is needed, but that it cannot carry out the policy-maker's function itself. Williams sets for himself what he describes as a "modest" task, in keeping with his conception of the philosopher's role as underlabourer: firstly, that of showing how the discipline of philosophical thinking can help us to become clear about fundamental issues in curriculum policy, and secondly, that of showing that while philosophy cannot tell us what we can and should teach, it can inform our reflections on these matters. In the course of his arguments, Williams questions more than a few commonly held assumptions, particularly in relation to issues such as assessment, the process/product distinction in debates about curriculum, the scope and limitations of the conventional post-primary curriculum, the merits of practical subjects, and the importance of personal and social education.

My own contribution, "Power, Partiality and the Purposes of Learning," arises from a concern that, amid the pluralism that reigns in most Western democracies, something which is recognisable as a new metaphysics — a more or less urbane metaphysics of power — has gained ascendancy in place of the once dominant metaphysics of

Christendom. I am keen to show that while there is nothing historically new about preoccupation with power and its pursuit, what *is* new is that this pursuit is now something which courts not merely the commitments of leaders in politics and business, it also attires itself as a belief system worthy of the convictions of each individual. More particularly, the concern underlying my contribution to the symposium is that the attitudes and practices increasingly engendered by educational effort, indeed which are all too often evident in the behaviour of educational authorities themselves, commend the metaphysics of power to the young in a tacit but relentless way; a way which is nevertheless becoming more blatant.

Where convictions are publicly professed as democratic, or liberal, or Christian, or whatever, it may seem odd to claim that the pursuit of power has become a dominant creed. But it is precisely the public character of professed beliefs that helps to disguise the influential play of the metaphysics of power. In the second part of my presentation, therefore, I attempt to make this metaphysics explicit by examining seven theses which contain its essentials. I then invite the participants, or the readers in this instance, to compare these theses, not so much with publicly professed convictions, but rather with the kinds of actions which attend discourse on policy matters and which seek to impose the constraints of partiality on decision-making in the public arena. In the final part I argue that the purposes of learning must, in some enduring and practical sense, be conceived *against* the metaphysics of power, and here I introduce five characteristics of dialogue to illustrate what the approach I am recommending looks like in practice. Continuing in this vein, I conclude with six theses of my own for defensible educatonal discourse and decision-making.

The theme of the symposium— partnership and the benefits of learning — suggests that these benefits are a public inheritance, as distinct from private goods or privileges to be purchased by individual consumers in an educational marketplace. The influence of market thinking in education is nevertheless immense in most Western democracies at present, although it is less pronounced in the Republic of Ireland than elsewhere. There are few schools in this country, however, which have not been touched in recent years by the spirit of active competition. There are many schools, moreover, which have embraced a market outlook and have sought to make a virtue of it in their practice.

INTRODUCTION 11

In such circumstances it is all too easy to lose the insight that the benefits of learning make themselves available most fully only where acquisitive and protectionist impulses have yielded to a special kind of solidarity. Unlike commodities, the benefits of learning increase by being shared. Sharing, however, presupposes a certain discipline, that of being able to give and being prepared to receive. And in education, this is not merely an interplay of information, but also of perspectives, insights and dispositions; an interplay which enables each participant to appreciate more fully his or her distinctive identity and which opens experience to new possibilities. Partnership, likewise, is not just a comforting avowal, it carries responsibilities whereby protectionist impulses must yield priority to some genuine commitment to dialogue and its practical consequences.

ECONOMICS, POLITICS AND THE PHILOSOPHY OF EDUCATION IN IRELAND

Barney O'Reilly

Introduction

Outlining the theme for this conference in a document sent to speakers, Dr. Hogan suggested that a philosophical phase in the current Irish education debate would provide "an opportunity to enable insights to become more inclusive; judgements to become more discerning; commitments to become more critically informed and defensible standpoints to become more explicit." This is a challenging agenda, and one in which I am happy to participate, on the understanding that sharing insights and critically examining our current judgements really does imply that present existing commitments are open to being modified; that standpoints currently defended, are open to being adjusted. I have to admit that I come to a philosophical discussion on education with some concern that the philosophising may be but another mode of defence, and have little of the openness to revision that our current dilemmas demand.[1]

In a more general sense, it is with some hesitation that I present myself among philosophers in a forum such as this because there is much in the world of philosophical discourse with which I am not familiar. I am a teacher and education administrator, rather than a philosopher. My primary interest is in helping learning happen, by attempting to assemble the environments, resources, general contexts and support, that facilitate the process. My primary concern is with praxis rather than "theoria." I also feel a little out of place in the company of my eminent co-panelists who are professional philosophers. So it is with some little trepidation that I make my contribution. In the title I have chosen I link economics and politics with the philosophy of education, for a number of reasons. Firstly, because of my particular role as a chief executive, I am acutely aware of the financial and economic dimensions of Irish education — about securing resources, trying to manage, seeking efficiency and effectiveness and watching costs and budgets. Secondly, because the vocational education system in which I work is quite explicit in its acknowledgments of the contribution of education to economic development, of the nexus that joins the education and economic systems, and is explicit also in acknowledging the role of education in the economic well being of the individual. The VEC system was established precisely on the broad premise that appropriate education can operate as a policy instrument in economic and social development, and plays a central role in influencing the economic prospects of individuals. Thirdly, because the VEC in its governance system is linked structurally with the local government framework, and hence with the party political system, it is to be expected that any "reflective practitioner" in such a context, would reflect on the wide range of issues that arise in that domain and out of these links. Of course, I should point out that "the politics of education" is not a matter confined to elected representatives and political parties or to VECs, no more than the economic role of education is confined to the vocational sector. All of the myriad management interests, from the Episcopate, the Association of Community and Comprehensive Schools, the Teacher Unions, the Parents' Councils, the CEOs, the Department of Education — all are active agents in the field of education politics. This casual observation about the politics of education brings me to a first reflection, or question, to philosophers and the academic community in general.

There is, quite properly, much concern to make explicit and to study the philosophy of education, but how, or why, is there so little academic reflection on either the politics or economics of education in Ireland? To the best of my knowledge there are at most two academic economists who specialise in economics in education.[2] I am not aware of any university education department or college of education that employs an economist. As far as I can make out, none of the interest groups think it necessary to engage economists, except on occasional exercises in the context of some particular campaign. The sustained analytical scrutiny of the sources and the application of resources to the educational endeavour is not a feature of our educational discourse. Neither are the processes of decision-making in education — the politics of education — the subject of sustained analytical scrutiny. It may be argued that much political analysis is carried out under the rubric of History or Sociology. History and politics have become increasingly discrete areas of academic enquiry in contemporary society. The study of politics as a discipline developed rapidly in recent decades,[3] but the study of the politics of education in Ireland is still very much of an untilled field, or at best secret garden, little analysed by theoreticians, and little understood by the general public.[4]

Contrast this relative obscurity, in which the politics and economics of education reside, with the lofty role afforded to philosophy and philosophers in our educational discourse. All courses, and every education faculty has its philosopher and philosophical element. As is proper, no teacher can escape the requirement to reflect philosophically on the nature, purposes and processes of education. But who studies the politics and the economics of education? And where can departmental officials, administrators, union or management leaders, school principals or concerned teachers and parents, find the academic underpinning for these dimensions of their work?[5]

It may be that this imbalance is but a skewed perception from my particular vantage point. I wish to argue, however, that there is an imbalance, firstly, in the absence of a discourse on the economics or the politics of education, and secondly, that within philosophical discourse there is a relative neglect to explore the philosophical questions that arise when the economics and politics of education are the subject of systematic study. I wish further to suggest that this imbalance seals off significant domains of educational reality from systematic public scrutiny and inhibits our capacity to respond adequately to the challenges for change which face the education service and the education system.[6] I must hasten to state that it is no part of my thesis to claim that philosophical reflection inhibits change or that philosophical discourse is in some way inimical to the fullest development of the education service. I am, rather, arguing that there is a delimitation of philosophical discourse to the exclusion of the more pragmatic, but equally fundamental, dimensions represented by economics and politics. I will attempt in this paper to outline a case for the significance of economic and political matters to the analysis of the education system, and to present reflections on some philosophical issues that appear to me to arise in such an analysis. Following this, I hope to present some thoughts on the implications for change in Irish education that arise from these reflections. I will explore briefly some common dimensions in philosophical discourse about education and similar discourse in the domains of economics and politics. I propose to argue that the advent of mass schooling over the last hundred and fifty years, being co-terminal with the growth of democratic political structures and the emergence of nation states on the one hand, and the dominance of market economic theory, on the other hand, is not a chance event but due to a deeply rooted relationship. This relationship has inevitably meant that the economic and political significance of contemporary education is central, not peripheral, to any philosophical understanding of it.

Discourse in Education, Politics and Economics — Common Roots in Modernity

It is necessary first to state that when discussing education and its philosophy, or indeed its politics and economics, my subject is the institution of schooling as a mode of education and the processes of education as they occur in that institutional context. In contemporary society, a philosophy of education must be a philosophy of schooling.[7] To remind ourselves of this distinction is to draw attention to a number of relevant parallels. The most significant one for our purposes is the timing of the development of those forms of classroom and school organisation we currently know, which were both made possible and were driven by the development of mass education. It was Adam Smith (1723-1790), Professor of Logic and Moral Philosophy at Glasgow University, who, in 1759, said that "Domestic education is the institution of nature; public education the contrivance of man."[8] It was the same Adam Smith who is credited with being the founding father of economics as an academic discipline and formulated the basic tenets of market economics. The parallel I point to is the emergence of the organisational framework of schooling and the systematic study of economic life over the same historical period. With David Hamilton (1989) I see, to a significant degree, the application of a related set of concepts, ideas and theories in both phenomena.[9] A second parallel is the emergence over the same time span of the basic ideas of democratic governance and politics and the emergence of cultural nationalism and nation states.

The upheavals of the late 18th and early 19th centuries, the American Revolution, the French Revolution, and the Industrial Revolution, signalled major revisions in the philosophical, ethical and economic criteria used to understand and to organise society. The establishment of the empiricist philosophical tradition of the Enlightenment meant the overthrow of medieval metaphysical explanations and theologically rooted accounts for either the physical or the moral domains. Newtonian physics had explained the physical world as a quasi-mechanical set of systematic relationships which were open to scrutiny by systematic empirical observation. It was a seemingly natural progression to uncover the parallel systems operating in the moral and social domains — which was the enterprise set out by Adam Smith in *The Wealth of Nations*(1759) and the *Theory of Moral Sentiments* (1776). In the economic market theories of Smith, the market with its "invisible hand" ensured that free interplay of individual self-interest, operating as market forces, produced the most effective and harmonious distribution of the goods of this world. The laws of economics are a sub-set of the laws of nature and the "good life" is pursued by living in accordance with them. The application of reason to economic phenomena can uncover the law of economics and point the direction for the good life.

This conception of an "out-there" system, the full understanding of the rules of which is necessary for the ordering of society to achieve the good life, is also implicit in the theoretical framework of Karl Marx (1818-1883). A central additional insight in Marxist economics is that it is not sufficient to consider only the material dimensions of the processes of production and exchange, one must also understand the *social* relations of production and exchange which are, for Marxists, the primary elements in the pursuit of the good life. Put crudely, for Smith and classical economists, to manage the processes of production and exchange efficiently will, *ipso facto,* lead to the optimum outcomes for individuals and society:

for Marx, priority must be afforded to the social relations in the processes of production and exchange in order to generate the good life. Despite this difference in emphasis, both marxist and classical economics share a perspective in which:

(a) well-being in terms of the relations of production and exchange is central to the notion of the good;

(b) this well-being is to be achieved by acting in accordance with the true laws of the economic system which are amenable to rational enquiry.

For Marx, progress is triggered by the unsatisfactory nature of the social relations of production which, by a process of dialectic, lead to their own replacement over time. For classical economists, progress is a process driven by the ever-present demand for rational efficiency in production and exchange.

Charles Taylor, in his book *Sources of the Self,* sees the emergence of the notion of an "economic system" and the systematic study which aims to uncover its laws, as part of a larger movement towards the "affirmation of ordinary life" which is, in his thesis, central to the culture of modernity.[10] The emergence of democratic systems of governance also, I suggest, can be linked to this "affirmation of the ordinary life" — affirmation of the ordinary individual as a source of moral and political authority. The slogans of the French Revolution — Liberty, Equality and Fraternity, (seem to me to) evoke the range of values which inhere also in the economic domain. Liberty and Equality are the basis of the free interplay of the market, as being the basis of the relationships between individuals in the state.

Classical economics put the emphasis on Liberty; Marxists stress Equality which they link with Fraternity, in both politics and economics. A core insight in Marxist politics is to stress the interrelatedness between the economic and the political. In the new democratic political doctrines, individual citizens are the sources of moral and political authority: by their consent they legitimate those organisations of state which are required in their functioning to recognise the source of their legitimation. The study of politics in democratic societies then, becomes a study of the systems by which society organises the interplay, the exchange, and the conflicts which arise from this moral and political authority, and from the consequent dignity and rights which are vested in individual citizens. Economics studies the system of production and exchange carried on in the service of material self interest. Politics studies the exchange of moral authority, the rights and the powers to govern, that occur in any social formation.[11]

A problem created by the shift in sources for political authority was the configuration of units within which groups of individuals would adhere politically — the question of state formation. The difficult and often turbulent processes by which some regions coalesced to form nation states such as France or Italy, and others hived off to establish separate nation states (such as Ireland, but not Wales or Scotland) is also an underlying dynamic in the nineteenth century, continuing into the twentieth century. The growing significance of *national* identity to the sense of self of modern man is an aspect of these centuries which cannot be ignored. The notion then that economic systems and political systems have co-terminal boundaries which allowed for their management, became a common place. So much so, that we now normally fail to advert to the extent to which a concept such as "the Irish economy" or "the French economy" are but recent constructs. A third major and linked development during this period was the slow but steady provision of public schooling for all the population. Slowly but steadily throughout the nineteenth and twentieth centuries, a system of schooling characterised by group or class instruction in publicly funded institutions developed. The emergence of these institutions was in direct response to changing economic and political conditions, driven by a new epistemology, a new economics and a new politics, which were transforming societies.[12]

Now the progressive establishment of public schooling throughout this period cannot be understood, but as intimately related to these developments. Some philosophical points in the nature of the relationship we will consider below. The point here is to note the broad range of social developments of which the emergence of schooling is a part. Now by pointing to the parallel emergence of schooling with democratic politics, national states, and modern economics, I am suggesting not just an accidental but an organic link in the relationship between schooling, economics and politics, a relationship which goes to the core of modern life. In doing that I am suggesting that philosophising about education and schooling is unreal if divorced for the political and economic milieu in which it occurs. I propose now to identify some of these linkages at the level of deeper structure.[13]

Theory in Education, Economics and Politics : Common Philosophical Status as "Practical Knowledge"

When working as a teacher educator, I was much exercised by the nature of the theoretical knowledge acquired and held by teachers and its relationship to their professional activities as teachers. I became interested in the Theory/Practice debate and worked my way into a series of reflections under the title "Theory and Common Sense and the Practical Knowledge of the Teacher" read to an ESAI Conference in 1986.

The basic insight I attempted to elaborate was that the theoretical knowledge-base of the practising teacher was best characterised as "practical knowledge." This "practical knowledge" of the teacher had more similarity with "common sense" in the manner in which it operated than it had with scientific theory.[14] My understanding of the practical knowledge of the teacher was shaped considerably by my (no doubt unsophisticated) understanding of the Aristotelian distinction between Techne & Phronesis and Episteme[15] and by Lonergan's concept of Common Sense knowledge.[16]

The dominant characteristic of practical knowledge, apart from its direct relationship to interpersonal social actions, is its provisional, uncompleted and open-ended nature. By this I mean that a teacher's understanding of any given professional-life situation does not issue automatically in an appropriate action. The teacher's actual action is always open to adjustment in the light of the answer to some further pertinent question she may ask about the concrete situation. However, if action is to be taken, the questioning has to stop at some point, and something done. The capacity to balance the need for further question and insight, against the requirement to "do something now," or more precisely, "respond appropriately now," is the characteristic of the reflective practitioner, the wise teacher operating with her practical knowledge.

I mention these reflections on the practical knowledge of the teacher, not so much for their own relevance but because of the extent to which my experience suggests that the practical knowledge of the administrator or manage, in dealing with the political or with economic dimensions of education, was of precisely the same type. The decision-making of teachers and of educational administrators, politicians and economists are isomorphic, I suggest. The factors to be examined, the range of theoretical understandings that are relevant, the concrete decisions to be made, may all be different. But the need to ask the broadest possible range of questions, and finally to make a decision in the full knowledge that some significant question may have been overlooked due to bias or just sloth, or the pressure of time, are common.[17] This is, no doubt, obvious to you philosophers as but a home-spun (and criminally cryptic and incomplete) dimension of the nature and status of the human sciences. The point for me is that the study of education and the study of economics and politics are each pursued to assist in decision-making, to yield *practical knowledge:* they each make similar demands for reflective rigour and are burdened with the prospect of incompleteness and the enigma that even to do nothing, is to do something. So the study of the philosophy of education is not really remote from philosophical reflections on political and economic matters. The same issues of epistemological status and relationship to action apply.

Now a frequent critique of modern society points to the growing dominance of technical rationalism or instrumental rationality and the charge is levelled that such a form of rationality is dehumanising. Technical rationality dehumanises by its attempts to objectify human predicaments and render them in terms of empirically measurable data: human dilemmas are reduced to means and techniques without reference to purposes and ends. The "manager" is presented as a character of this technical-rational culture, whose mode of address to practical issues represents "the obliteration of the distinction between manipulative and non-manipulative social relations."[18] It is my contention that neither educators nor education administrators are tied to a form of practical knowledge in which the philosophical questions are held not to be pertinent. I see no reason to assume that either the economics of education or its politics are less stringent in their validity tests and less open to having their assumptions subjected to philosophical analysis.[19] This line of argument may have little weight other than to show that reflection about economics and politics is not inherently remote, or different in kind from reflections on education, and that I have experienced this commonality at different times in the course of my own career. But I wish now to argue a stronger link and to claim that philosophical reflections on education which do not address the political and the economic are incomplete and a disservice to the process of education.

Ideological Uses of the Philosophy of Education

To ease my way into this stronger argument, I wish to contrast the terms "philosophy," "ideology" and "rhetoric" as used to describe ideas propounded about education, (or indeed politics and economics). To speak of the "ideology(ies) of education" as opposed to the philosophy or philosophies of education signals a more "engaged" disposition for those taking part in the discourse. To refer to an ideology of education invites an audience to adopt a critical stance in respect of the concepts and theoretical framework being advanced. Depending on your position, then you might, for example, speak of a "Catholic ideology of education" and a "Marxist philosophy of education" or *vice versa,* depending on the direction you wished to cast a disparaging glance.[20] It is possible, on the other hand, to deny the negative dimension to the concept of ideology and to claim that both it (and philosophy) should be used as neutral descriptive concepts.[21] Of course, if you really wish to be pejorative about the ideational framework of another, it is referred to as "rhetoric," implying that the arguments are being utilised to shield the true purposes or basis of a position taken or an action proposed, or that the ideas and arguments are calculated to engage the support of some who would demur if the basis were fully and forthrightly stated. (Or to use Chomsky's telling phrase, "manufacturing consent" for the optics).

In drawing this distinction I am focusing attention on the political potential of philosophical discourse. To suggest that philosophy has such a potential is not to claim that "a disinterested desire to know" is either impossible or that philosophers are operating to an agenda. It is not an imputation of motives to any philosopher. But I do hold, that their being-in-the-world for most philosophers includes a deep-seated desire/aspiration to influence the world with their lives and with their philosophy — to make a difference, however modest. In addition, from the organisational dynamics of the traditions or groups in which individuals carry out their reflections and their philosophising, there arises a need to articulate the self-understandings of that tradition or group, as a justification, and in the interests of its survival, growth and development. These sources of engagement, one individual and one social, do not inherently invalidate or undermine the analyses presented by philosophers, but their presence does invite the critical appraisal or interrogation of their audience.[22]

So one of my first critical observations is to suggest that philosophers of education have unduly restricted the scope of their explorations. I am contending that philosophical reflections on education focus on a range of issues, and by neglecting others, inhibit or make more difficult the processes of change. I wish to suggest that philosophers of education are concerned with three main sets of issues.[23]

Firstly, epistemological issues which are examined, primarily, in the context of curriculum, yielding views and positions about such practical matters as: the nature, types and the classifications of knowledge, what constitutes an appropriate balance in curriculum and the pedagogical implications of such understandings.[24] The second set are issues relating to inter-subjectivity — the nature of inter-subjective relationships, especially discourse, with particular reference to the implications for pupil-teacher relationships, and significantly for my purposes, with implications for the role of culture or ethos in the socialisation process.[25] The third set of issues I identify may not be, in any real sense, discrete from the proceeding ones but are separated by me because they are directly open to issues of the role of religion in life. I refer to them as "theological issues" because they seem rooted in questions of a "vertical relationship" between man and God as a response to questions about purpose and meaning in life.[26]

Now I do not wish to devalue the significance of these issues, but I do suggest that concerns about ethos, for example, are most frequently addressed within a framework of argumentation about the appropriateness of particular governance arrangements for schooling. In curriculum matters philosophers are almost universally arguing for redressing the balance in favour of the humanities, interpretative studies or the liberal curriculum. Even more particularly, philosophical analysis of the place of religion in education usually leads to, or is pointed towards, conclusions about the rights and role of church groupings in the organisation/provision of schooling systems. I have no reservations about this, and freely acknowledge that such philosophising is used to reach competing views on these practical matters, and am happy to take my place in such disputations. My primary concern here is to broaden the scope of the discourse which is relevant to these issues and to argue for the legitimacy of concerns from the domains of economics and politics from "ordinary life," in this discourse, particularly as it is engaged in by philosophers.[27]

Education and Economics and Politics

Specifically, I seek acknowledgement in philosophical discourse of the following dimensions of schooling, which, it appears to me, are rooted in the economic functions of schools and schooling systems:

- Schools contribute to the common good by contributing to the material well-being and the economic productivity of individuals and society.

- Efficiency in the application of resources for specified ends is a central guiding value in the conduct of schooling, which requires to be balanced with concern for equality, liberty and community solidarity.

- Among the non-optional functions of schools and schooling systems the following socio-economic functions are:
    - the formation of productive skills;
    - the sorting of human resources;
    - the regulation of labour force flows.

It is my contention that these are unavoidable functions of schooling. To exclude them from philosophical discourse on contemporary education is to truncate that discourse. To belittle their significance as "the rehabilitation of cupidity endorsed by secularisation" (as I understand P. Hogan to say) reflects an unwillingness to affirm ordinary life.[28] No school, or group of schools, is outside the operation of these functions. Claims by schools to treat these functions as unworthy or irrelevant, are a denial. School type differentiations at second level, between secondary schools and vocational schools, have been created and perpetuated, in large measure, as a direct response to perceptions about the functions of schooling in the labour market.[29] The processes by which the differences between these school types have been eroded (to a significant extent) are significantly related to changing perceptions about the needs of the labour market and the appropriate organisation of schools to respond to it.[30]

If examination and certification systems fail to provide the service of distinguishing people on criteria which are acceptable as a basis for assigning either places in further education or actual vacancies in the labour market, then those certification systems will be stood down.[31] To assert so is not to claim exclusive priority for the economic functions of schooling; it is to contend that economic functions cannot be effectively ignored and ought to be the subject of careful scrutiny. To decry the pursuit of "ordinary goods" for philosophic or for religious reasons is to lose touch with a pivotal reality (not the only reality) of life. The failure to affirm the ordinary, leads to much educational philosophy being ignored as "irrelevant," except as ideology or rhetoric.

Turning to politics, I suggest that a bedrock value or a "constitutive good" in a democratic state is *equality:* the mandate to govern in democratic states, rests fundamentally on the decisions of the governed. Even if given only at elections, the right to govern is conferred by the people. In addition, the central basis of a state's ongoing legitimacy is intimately related to its showing equal concern and respect for each person in its dealings.[32]

On this island two new states have been established in the course of this century. Philosophers of education should be in a position to reflect deeply on the relationship between state formation and schooling systems. We do not appear to have done that.

There appears to me to be two central difficulties facing any state, or would be state, in its self-preservation. The first, which is particularly apparent to us on this island, with our experience, relates to the demarcation between the state and other states. The processes of state formation on this island between the late 18th century up to the declaration of the Irish Republic in 1948, and on again to 1968, right up to current events, in which people were mobilised, identities cultivated, institutions dismantled and institutions built up, have been intimately linked to the dynamics of the schooling systems.[33] My question is — how did, and does, the schooling system knit into these processes of identity building, mobilisation, contestation and institution building?

The second major difficulty facing a state relates to the management of its internal interest cleavages, the sectional interests which arise from the economic and social and cultural disparities, created by history. When planning this paper I had thought I would outline a framework scheme of the functioning of the school system in respect of these two political roles of the state. I am, however, forced to acknowledge that this is too ambitious a project for the space available and indeed, for my meagre capacity. I must content myself with a number of observations and questions to act as pointers to issues which, I suggest, require philosophical analysis.

- Do differences of religion in all circumstances and irrespective of other concerns, always warrant the support of different systems of education?

- Do differences in social class, ability, employment destination, or even gender, warrant differences in institutional provision?

- Are cultural, quasi-ethnic differences (such as those identified by travellers, or argued to differentiate Catholics from Protestants in Northern Ireland) sufficient to justify/demand specific institutional provision.

In short, on what basis is a state justified/obliged in attempting to minimise the impact of differences, through the education system? (I grapple with a practical version of this abstract question when striving to respond to the education needs of traveller children, attempting to respect cultural diversity while also attempting to create economic opportunity). Are all cultural differences to be cherished, cultivated, institutionalised? by employment destination? by gender? by cultural/ethnic group? by religion? What is the role of the schooling system in the promotion of civic culture and the democratic character and allegiance of citizens? If I may be so bold as to propose an agenda to philosophers of education, it is an exploration of the philosophical issues arising from these questions of the interfaces of schooling with the political and the economic. The tensions between the espousal of core values such as equality, efficiency and freedom of choice are inescapable in the day to day realities of schooling, whether we are in classrooms, in principals' offices, at administrators' desks or at legislators' chairs. We cannot but be content; we have no option but to strike balances. In the funding decisions we make, in the decisions about structures that we make, *as well* as in our personal interactions, the balances we strike between our values become lived realities.

Conclusion

I propose to conclude with two observations. The first of these concerns the concept of "man's integration" and the second concerns forms of social organisation which I believe to be dysfunctional in contemporary Ireland. Margaret Archer, outlining a theoretical framework to describe the evolution of educational systems, employed the concept of *Mono-Integration* to describe the position of schooling systems which, while performing a *wide range of functions* in society, are governed by mechanisms which integrate schools within the organisational framework of *one of these functions*. If schools were owned and run by the associated banks and/or trade unions, then they are mono-integrated with their economic functions. The form of mono-integration Archer identified in 19th century Europe, was between the schooling system and churches as organisations, so that the primary functions reflected in the governance systems of the schools related to the role of schools in the religious life of peoples and the organisational life of the churches, as aids to catechetics and denominational affiliation. Such mono-integration, I believe, is a significant characteristic of the first and second level schooling systems on this island which, in their governance systems, are mono-integrated in ways which afford dominance to the religious partnership element in the education project, by integrating schools predominantly with church organisations. The VEC as a system labours under a parallel, if opposite form of partial integration with the economic and political system, which also is an impoverishment. It appears to me that a partnership for the benefit of schooling, for the benefit of learning and for the benefit of society, requires that we move away from our partial and fragmented systems and integrate the governance of our schooling system with the totality of the social functions it aspires to in our society. In this respect I have argued that the relative neglect of philosophical reflection on the economic and political nexus between schooling and society is unhelpful and needs to be addressed.

For my second observation I wish to focus on the major social and political challenge which faces this island and about which recent events have given us some reason for optimism. I have been suggesting in this paper a firm relationship between schooling system and nation/state identity. As states and communities in these islands seek to articulate new institutional mechanisms, new ways to supersede conflict arising from cultural identity by the reworking of these identities; as concepts of human solidarity and cohesion are invoked which over-arch, while respecting the identities that generated the conflict, I ask: what are the implications for schooling systems? My own assessment is that schooling systems organised on denominational and culturally divided/mono-integrated lines are dysfunctional in a contemporary Ireland attempting to bridge the gaps that exist between communities.

This observation amounts to a suggestion that the process of educational reform in the Republic cannot proceed without reference to the broad political context in which it is to take place. I cannot but think, with irony, that the last major attempt to restructure Irish education took place in 1919, in the throes of the events from which the divided states on this island emerged. Some of the present ferment for educational reform in the Republic can only be explained by a broader national groping for a new conception of Irishness, a new concept of citizenship which allows us to overreach those differences which are linked with religious affiliation. Failure to acknowledge this will, I suggest, impoverish the debate on educational reform and stunt our prospects for building a school system adequate to the complexities of contemporary Ireland. for this to happen philosophers of education must, I suggest, include in their subject matter those questions which arise from the linkages between economics and politics and education. An affirmation of these ordinary linkages does not imply a neglect of others but, in the title to the conference, a partnership for the benefits of learning.

IRISH EDUCATIONAL POLICY:
THE PLACE OF RELIGION IN A PLURALIST SOCIETY

Eoin G. Cassidy

Introduction

When the period of consultation arising from the publication of the 1992 Green Paper *Education for a Changing World* commenced some three years ago there was much comment on the serious implications for Irish educational policy of the lack of a debate on a philosophy of education.[1] In that short period much has changed for the better. For example, one cannot but welcome the thought provoking contribution of the current Minister for Education, Ms. Niamh Bhreathnach in her John Marcus O'Sullivan Memorial (Tralee) lecture "Towards a Coherent Philosophy of Education,"[2] the detailed attention given to this issue in the *Report on the National Education Convention (NEC)*, and, finally, this present worthy initiative by the Educational Studies Association of Ireland. The debate so far has tended, quite naturally, to focus on the disquieting absence of a clearly articulated philosophy underlying government policy on education. It is time to move beyond that position and to state how we would envisage the shape of a philosophy of education which could underpin Irish educational legislation at the close of the twentieth century.

This paper is an attempt to address this issue within the confines of the title "The place of religion in a pluralist society." What we will pursue in this paper is a philosophical analysis of the extent to which religion is recognised in the Green Paper and the extent to which the forthcoming White Paper and, in turn, the proposed Education Act could, or should, give recognition to religion in the educational system. In addressing the question of the place of religion in a pluralist society I am taking religion in the broad sense of that term to include a discussion of the place of religious values and ideals which, while foundational to all of the mainstream Christian denominations, are not exclusive to Christianity, and many of which are shared by those of no religious persuasion.

A call for transparency

The Green Paper's attitude to the religious dimension of its subject has provoked many commentaries, the most outstanding being Bruce Bradley's "Ghostly Rhythms: Philosophy and Religion in Irish Education."[3] This study is worthy of comment both for its trenchant criticism of the Green Paper and its carefully reasoned argumentation. Bradley highlights the fact that in the course of the 240-page document religion merits only the most cursory of mention and even that, for the most part, is by way of emphasising the rights of parents who do not wish to have their children receive religious education. And he notes that where religion is specified, as it is in the Junior Cycle curriculum, there is no attempt to offer a rationale for its presence. This omission is in marked contrast to the treatment of subjects such as Art, Music and Physical Education. He further observes that in the Green Paper's treatment of the importance of fostering an appreciation of our cultural heritage there is not a single mention of the role which religion, in particular Christianity, has played in shaping and/or fostering Irish culture — a quite astonishing omission to the mind of anyone with even the most superficial knowledge of Irish history.

Whatever about the value of Bradley's observations on the minimalist treatment of religion in the Green Paper, the importance of his article lies in the way in which it directly confronts the lack of consistency which marks the underlying philosophy of education in the Green Paper. In particular he highlights the lack of a clear congruence between the philosophy of education, as enunciated in the section entitled Aims of Education, and the rest of the document.[4] Even where the Minister for Education in her Tralee lecture and the *Report on the NEC* attempt to redress the narrow utilitarian bias of the Green Paper in favour of the Classical Liberal model of education, (which, with its more humanistic focus, would be more open to the place of religion in education) Bradley says that "the suspicion endures, however, that Philosophy of Education is being viewed largely as a detachable, add-on statement of ideals, rather than an explication of practice."[5] It is not hard to have a certain sympathy for Bradley's standpoint. For example, from the point of view of the place of religion on the curriculum, the spiritual and moral development of the student does receive recognition in the "Aims of Education" section,[6] but only disappointment would result from a search of either the Green Paper, the Tralee lecture or the *Report on the NEC* for even the briefest treatment of the rationale behind these aims and/or the way in which they are to be realised in and through the curriculum. In the absence of such a development of these ideals the suspicion must indeed be that they are, at best, pious aspirations which have no real bearing on the thrust of Irish educational policy.

Why should there be a concern with the lack of a detailed treatment in the Green Paper of the rationale behind the presence of religion on the curriculum? For instance, there is no such detailed treatment in the Green Paper of the place of Mathematics or English. Furthermore, it is doubtful whether this issue would have been a concern fifty, or even twenty-five, years ago. The rationale for the presence of religion on the curriculum would have been taken for granted — presumed to have been self-evident and thus unnecessary to state. However, as is becoming evident even to the most casual observer, Irish culture has changed radically in the last twenty-five years and is continuing to change in ways that are increasingly affecting society's perception of the value and place of religion in people's lives and thus the value and place of religion in the school curriculum. In consequence, although the results of the most recent census reveal that ninety four per cent of the population profess to be believing Christians, it may, nevertheless, be increasingly difficult to presume on a clear understanding and general acceptance of the importance of religion on the school curriculum. This alone would suggest the need for a thorough treatment of the rationale for the presence of religion on the curriculum in a document of such importance as the Green Paper. However, there is an altogether more pressing reason for a rationale and this emerges from the way in which the Green Paper itself has suggested significant changes to the manner in which religion is situated on the curriculum. The change is primarily a change of emphasis, but one that is profound and pervasive despite being produced by virtual silence rather than concrete proposals. The change of emphasis is so obvious that one might wonder whether those who framed the document were intent on overturning some of the more important societal values reflected in the practice of education since the foundation of the state. Let me give an example; the Primary School Curriculum, published as recently as 1971, contained in its treatment of religion on the curriculum the following statement:

> Of all the parts of a school curriculum Religious Instruction is by far the most important, as its subject-matter, God's honour and service, includes the proper use of all man's faculties, and affords the most powerful inducements to their proper use.[7]

The contrast with the treatment of religion in the Green Paper could not be more clear-cut. In its treatment of the primary school curriculum the Green Paper states merely that provision is made in the curriculum and school timetable for religious instruction.[8] There is not a single reference either to the value or the importance of religion on the curriculum. Furthermore, the briefest perusal of the sections dealing with the aims and functions of the primary school curriculum in the two documents reveals an equally stark contrast regarding the place given to religion.[9] That this change in emphasis regarding the place of religion in the school curriculum is not something which is confined simply to the primary sector is evidenced by the failure either to offer any educational rationale for the presence of religion at the Junior Cycle level or to situate it among the list of core subjects to be studied at this level,[10] and most surprising of all the omission of any reference whatsoever to religion in the treatment of the Senior Cycle, something which is in marked contrast to the most recent NCCA document on the Senior Cycle.[11] Whatever about the merits of any of the above suggested changes and/or changes of emphasis in respect of the place of religion on the school curriculum, one can have a certain sympathy with those who find it unacceptable that there has been no attempt in the Green Paper to offer a rationale that would offer clear guidelines regarding current Department of Education thinking on the place of religion in schools.

The issue at stake here is that of transparency. One of the most significant and praiseworthy features of the current debate on the future of Irish education is that it has been marked by a determined effort to dialogue with all interested parties on all issues in an open and frank manner.[12] Unfortunately, in this one area which concerns the place of religion on the curriculum, we still await evidence of this commitment.

Those responsible for the preparation of a White Paper and for the framing of an Education Act must work to preserve what is best in our society's inheritance, while at the same time engaging in constructive dialogue with changing cultural modes. The emergence of an increasingly enterprise orientated society, one which gives priority to the consumerist/materialist values of the market place, the increasing evidence in line with most Western "developed" countries of a more secular and religiously pluralist society, and finally, an increasing tendency to suggest a link between denominational education and sectarianism — a legacy of twenty-five years of violence in Northern Ireland, are but three of the more obvious developments which are contributing to the shaping of Irish culture and which pose challenges both to those who value religious belief and equally to those who are entrusted with framing legislation in the field of education.

Now, it is not the concern of this paper either to undertake a detailed analysis of these changes, or to offer a value judgement on them, or to assess their effects on the esteem in which Irish people hold religious belief. However, it is important to acknowledge openly the fact of these and other changes and to recognise that they pose a challenge to those concerned with charting the future of Irish educational policy, a challenge which has particular relevance to the place and status of religion on the curriculum. In the sections where the Green Paper treats of the challenges facing Irish education[13] there is, unfortunately, no awareness of this particular and most pressing challenge. Subsequent statements by the Minister for Education, the submission made by the Department of Education to the NEC and the *Report on the NEC* itself, show a recognition of the importance of the task posed for educationalists by the increasing evidence of religious pluralism in Ireland.[14] However, a thorough treatment of the rationale for the presence of religious education on the school curriculum at Primary level, Junior Cycle and Senior Cycle level is a task which still awaits to be tackled, and in the context of the changes in Irish society, needs to be tackled.

Difficulties facing educationalists

At the outset it must be recognised that there are genuine difficulties facing educationalists in attempting to offer a rationale for the place of religion in the schools — difficulties which arise from the very nature of religious belief and which are not shared to the same extent by other subjects on the curriculum. It is important that these be openly acknowledged.

Firstly, there is disagreement on the truth claims of religion and the value of religion for society and the individuals which make up society. There are those who are convinced that religious belief is of the utmost importance for personal and communal fulfilment. Equally there are those atheists or agnostics, albeit a very small percentage, approximately 5% of Irish society, who either deny or doubt the truth claims of religious belief and who in consequence may, to a lesser or greater extent, regard religion as harmful to societal progress and human fulfilment. In addition there are those who, while they may regard themselves as religious believers, are slow to recognise the relevance of religious belief for adult life in the contemporary secular western world. This latter category of person may very well see a value in religious education for children at primary school and Junior Cycle levels, in that it can offer a secure context for the acquiring of a necessary moral framework for adult life. However, the uniquely religious insights into the spiritual character of human life and/or the specifically Christian emphasis on the importance of developing a personal relationship with a loving God are perceived as being of little significance in terms of the quest for human fulfilment.

Secondly, there is disagreement on the epistemological status of religion and its appropriateness as a subject for a school curriculum. It is unnecessary to restate the well-known arguments popularised by positivists and given respectability in educational circles during the 1960s. However, it must be recognised that despite the many philosophical question marks poised over the idea of a world populated by neutral objective facts, there are some even today who, in agreement with the viewpoint of positivism, would consign religious education to the "Sunday School" on the basis that religion classes teach faith and that schools teach facts. More pertinently in the Irish context, there are some, such as the INTO in its 1991 document "The Place of Religious Education in the National School System," and repeated in its submission to the NEC forum in Dublin Castle, who make a distinction between religious instruction and religious education in order to question whether the idea of nurturing a child in a particular faith, as distinct from teaching about religion, should be the concern of schools, in particular those schools which are in receipt of state aid.[15] Finally, there are those who would object to religion on the curriculum on moral grounds, in that, in their view religious instruction/education is a form of indoctrination, something generally regarded as being at variance with the ideal of education and compromising the inalienable human right to freedom of thought and expression. Clearly, it does not need to be stressed that there are many who would argue that the epistemological status of religious instruction/education that is implied in these criticisms represents a gross distortion.[16]

Thirdly, there is the disagreement which focuses on the character of religious education, on whether religious education should be denominational or multi-denominational. There are those who would criticise the denominational character of religious education in the majority of Irish schools on the basis that there is always the danger of denominational education being, or becoming, sectarian. Pointing in particular to the religious dimension of the conflict in Northern Ireland, they would question whether denominational religious education has the capacity to teach not only a tolerance of, but also an understanding and respect for religious diversity.[17] Equally there are those who, from the opposite point of view, would argue that religious education which was not denominational in character, would fail to give due recognition to the faith community out of which every child's faith emerges and thus would render it difficult to facilitate students to grow in an appreciation of and commitment to their faith community. The emphasis in this argument is that religious education can never be reduced to 'knowledge' about religious belief without in some way compromising the very essence of religious belief which in all cases involves a commitment in the Christian religions to a personal relationship with a creative and loving God experienced in and through the faith community which is the Church.[18]

Fourthly, there is the disagreement which has its basis in an understanding of the nature of a modern democratic state and the extent to which the Churches should be free to manage schools and set guidelines for the ethos of the schools under their management. This issue focuses on the question of democratic accountability. From one side the view is expressed that the present system which, particularly at primary level, places a large measure of control in the hands of the various religious denominations, is inherently anti-democratic. It is not democratic because those effectively running the schools are acting without any mandate from the electorate.[19] From the other side there are those who would question the validity of this argument. They would make the point that the Church is not an alien structure external to the democratic life of the country, existing in independence and isolation from the people who constitute the local community; on the contrary, the vast majority of citizens/parents belong not just to the local community of a particular electoral area, but also voluntarily choose to belong to a local worshipping community i.e. the local Church. Furthermore, it is precisely the Church which gives expression to the ideals, values, and aspirations of the majority of the parents who have the primary responsibility for their children's education. Consequently, they argue that it would be strange, and indeed undemocratic, if the education system, which is so intimately concerned with the transmission of the ideals, values and aspirations of a community to the next generation, was somehow to exclude that institution/community whose very purpose is to give expression to this dimension to life.[20]

Clearly, this issue of democratic control/accountability is not directly connected to the question of the place of religion on the curriculum but it would be naive to suggest, in the context of the current debate on the future of Irish education, that the two issues are not in some way linked. The question ought to be honestly addressed as to whether the minimal treatment of religion on the curriculum in the Green Paper is to any extent motivated by a desire to counter-balance what is regarded by some as the excessive power of the Churches in the education system. From the opposite point of view it could be argued that the Churches' insistence on maintaining managerial control over parish-based primary schools has been strengthened by the belief that Department of Education policy on the place of religion on the curriculum has in recent years undergone a fairly major revision in favour of a system of values whose thrust is to marginalize or privatise religious belief.

The challenge posed by pluralism

In opening his article "Pluralism Revisited" (*Studies*, Summer 1994), Paul Andrews S.J. comments: "It may seem odd to write a defence of pluralism: like leaping to the defence of democracy. Nobody attacks it but people understand it in different ways."[21] This perception seems to be endorsed by the wide variety of approaches to pluralism that is evident in the submissions to the NEC. There is an almost universal welcome for a more pluralist educational environment, but the ways in which this ideal pluralist environment is described could not, in some cases, be more different. For some, the ideal would be one where religious education became synonymous with the study of comparative religion and where the integrated curriculum and all the component parts that combine to form the school ethos were modified in such a manner as not only to respect but to value equally the full range of diverse belief systems, theistic and non-theistic alike. For others, the ideal pluralist environment would represent roughly what exists at present i.e., the freedom and state support for the religious denominations and others (primarily those in the Educate Together movement and the Gaelscoileanna) to build and run schools in accordance with their beliefs.[22] For others, a pluralist environment would be one which gave minority groups real and affordable access at all levels to educational establishments which respected their beliefs and/or traditions.[23] For others, a pluralist educational environment would be one in which there would be the possibility of offering in the schools, through religious education among other things, an alternative to the contemporary all-embracing, one-dimensional, consumer-led and market-driven enterprise culture propagated by the media and advocated in educational documents such as the Green Paper.[24]

What the exponents of these four examples and the proponents of the numerous variations on these models have in common is the shared conviction that either present educational practices, or proposed educational developments, should be altered to provide for a genuinely pluralist educational environment. However, it is equally clear that the word pluralism by itself does not provide the best key which will allow us either to chart the most advantageous course for the future of Irish educational policy, or, in keeping with the much more limited focus of this paper, to discern the rightful place for religion on the curriculum.

In examining the notion of pluralism it must, firstly, be acknowledged that from a purely philosophical point of view, a pluralist society cannot convincingly lay claim to be morally superior to a homogeneous society. Openness and tolerance are not virtues which are necessarily the monopoly of a pluralist society. What is sometimes overlooked is that the contemporary liberal democracies which are commonly presumed to embody a pluralist ethos can in some respects be quite intolerant. For example, there is little tolerance in many contemporary liberal democracies of those who would question the values of an enterprise culture or of those who would question the adequacy of a utilitarian morality. However, the question of the superiority, or otherwise, of the contemporary liberal democracies is really beside the point because, like it or not, Ireland has become such a society. What is even more to the point is to acknowledge that in the contemporary Irish psyche a pluralist society has come to be associated with one which is committed to the principles of unity in diversity, tolerance and mutual respect. The growing commitment of Irish people to pluralism, as understood in this context, is undoubtedly of great significance and something which all educationalists must welcome and endeavour to foster.

In the context of the forthcoming education legislation, arguments as to the value or limitations of a homogeneous society are largely academic. In a modern democracy such as that which pertains in Ireland today, pluralism in the purely technical use of that term is simply a fact of life. Nevertheless, the extent of that pluralism must not be exaggerated. If the uncritical assumption of the homogeneous nature of Irish society which underpinned much thinking on education during the early years of the state was an inaccurate reflection of the actual state of society at that time; similarly we must not today presume that contemporary Irish society is in every respect radically pluralist in character. There is evidence to suggest that, in at least two important respects, contemporary Irish society is remarkably homogeneous, namely, the adherence of Irish people to the Christian faith, and their acceptance of many of the priorities which underpin the culture of the capitalist and consumer orientated Western developed world.

To what extent is the state committed to respecting diversity? What, if any, are the limits of its commitment to tolerating and/or respecting pluralism? Should the state be in the business of encouraging a pluralist society and, if so, to what extent? The first thing to be noted is that modern liberal democracies are founded on the desire to promote tolerance and to accommodate, in so far as is practical, a pluralism of values, ideals religious beliefs, etc. In this context, and having regard to the recent course of Irish history, those responsible for framing Irish legislation are obliged to respect a certain pluralism and, in particular, to foster an ethos of unity in diversity, tolerance and mutual respect — ideals associated with a pluralist society. However, unless one is prepared to accept anarchy and/or an extreme form of moral relativism/subjectivism there must be limits on the unqualified acceptance of pluralism. Apart from the existence of a substantial segment of the population who would reject unbridled pluralism on religious and/or social grounds, the most obvious limit on the acceptance of this extreme version of pluralism is to be found in our obligation to respect both the constraints of the Constitution and those international treaties which we have signed, particularly those associated with our membership of the United Nations and the European Union. In respect of education legislation in general, one must recognise the importance of those conventions on Human Rights and the Rights of the Child to which Ireland is a signatory.[25]

Regarding the issue of religious education one can hardly overestimate the importance of the Irish Constitution. Even the most cursory examination of the references to religion in the Green Paper would alert one to the fact that the Constitution will exercise a major determining force on the way in which religion is treated in any forthcoming legislation.[26] In a democratic society this is the way it should be. The problem is that interpreting the relevant articles in the Constitution has proved to be extremely problematical.[27] Although a discussion of the constitutional issues relating to religion in the schools is outside the scope of this paper it is, nevertheless, salutary to note the following areas which are controversial, or at least perceived in some circles to be controversial; areas such as the funding of privately-run religious schools and denominational teacher-training colleges, the funding of school chaplains and catechists, the provision of funding for inservice education for the teachers of religion, and the inclusion of religion in the integrated primary school curriculum. What is unfortunate is that concern over these issues — particularly the latter and the one which relates to the right of parents to remove their children from the religion class — have tended to dominate discussion of the place of religion in the schools to the detriment of any serious discussion of the really central issue, namely, the place and value of religion in the curriculum. In its concern to address the legal status of religious education in the curriculum the Green Paper has neglected almost totally to treat of the prior question of the rationale for the very presence of religion on the curriculum.

Searching for a rationale

In justifying proposals for the place of any subject on the curriculum there are two fundamental questions which must be answered satisfactorily, questions which transcend the more obvious issues of the intrinsic merit of the subject and the desire of parents to see the subject included on the curriculum. They can be expressed as follows: does the subject meet the criteria for the existence of an educationally valid subject area, and, to what extent is the subject capable of providing a forum in which commonly accepted aims of education may be brought to fruition? Regarding the place of religion on the curriculum the first of these questions reminds one of the seriousness of the allegations that religious education, particularly denominational religious education, is a form of indoctrination, and that it is inherently divisive or sectarian. Secondly, there is the less pejorative, but equally damaging allegation that the faith character of religious belief renders it ineligible to be included on the school curriculum, particularly the integrated model which pertains at primary level. The expressed viewpoint is that it is not possible to integrate secular and non-secular subjects because they are based on fundamentally different principles. The second question forces us to examine the importance, or otherwise, of religion on the curriculum with respect to meeting society's expectations for education. It is only in the context of a response to these two questions that one can adequately identify the place of religion in a school curriculum. What is regrettable about the debate so far on the place of religion on the curriculum is the failure to recognise the importance of these two issues.

In examining the place of religion in a pluralist society it is important, firstly, to acknowledge the recognition which is accorded in contemporary democracies to the legitimate expression of pluralism. In both the Green Paper and the *Report on the NEC* one finds an acceptance of this important feature of educational practice.[28] As the Green Paper states it:

> The proposed aims are likely to find expression in different forms and with varying degrees of emphasis, in accordance with the wishes of parents and the related ethos and traditions of the school.[29]

This recognition of legitimate pluralism acknowledges that within certain defined limits (setting a requirement for a minimum number of hours per week for the teaching of a subject) individual schools have the freedom to determine the status of a subject such as religious education on their curriculum in terms of their assessment of its intrinsic merits. This assessment will clearly be influenced by the particular ethos of the school. However, the justification for state support for the presence of any subject on the curriculum, including religious education, ultimately depends on a reasonable consensus on the part of society that the subject is capable of being explained in ways that meet the concerns expressed in the two questions posed above.

Responding to the criticisms of religious education

Regarding the contentions that religious education is a form of indoctrination and that it is inherently divisive or sectarian, all one can say is that these allegations reveal a vision of religious education and an understanding of the main Christian churches which does little justice to the contemporary facts. The ecumenical dialogue which embraces most of the main Christian denominations and indeed extends beyond the boundaries of Christianity, is testimony to an inclusive rather than an exclusive vision of truth. Furthermore, regarding the Roman Catholic Church, even the most cursory reading of either the Vatican II document on religious liberty,[30] or the more recent document *The Religious Dimension of Education in a Catholic*

School[31] would reveal a vision of religious education that could hardly be further removed from one that is susceptible to the charge of indoctrination.

A second contention that requires analysis is the suggested distinction between fact and faith, which would lead to the denial of the educational validity of a curriculum which seeks to integrate secular and non-secular subjects. What is the precise nature of this distinction? Is it meant to suggest that secular truths are empirically verifiable whereas religious truths are not open to such verification? But the idea that there is some neutral, factual, value-free realm of objectivity from which to teach subjects such as music, art, history and literature is, as any good teacher will confirm, highly questionable. Even in the scientific areas the distinction between fact and faith is not as clear-cut as was often presumed. The writings of philosophers of science such as Karl Popper and Thomas Kuhn offer us a far more nuanced and sophisticated vision of the complex relation which exists between facts and faith than that suggested by the earlier positivist understanding of scientific truth. Furthermore, to suppose that religious education exists in some type of fideist environment that is immune from the challenge of the questions posed by human experience is to misunderstand radically the nature of religious education and religious belief. All subjects which seek to understand and interpret reality are subject to the truth, and their claims stand or fall on that basis; religious belief is no exception.

Finally, one has to address a related issue, namely, the contention that religious education cannot properly be included in a school curriculum because, unlike any secular subject, it includes in its aims the fostering of commitment to a body of beliefs and practices. While religious believers would not deny that religious education cannot be reduced to knowledge about religion without in some way compromising the very essence of religious belief, nevertheless, they would be concerned to point out that the primary and overriding commitment in religious education/instruction, as in all subjects, is the commitment to the truth. Religious education not only testifies to the importance of an intellectual understanding and critical appreciation of the truth, it also testifies to the importance of a commitment to the truth. As would be recognised by most educationalists, it is only this commitment of the will, as well as the intellect to the truth, that can liberate and thus truly educate a person.

In consequence, just as moral education can never be equated with value clarification, but rather, seeks as one of its aims a commitment to the practice of a virtuous life, likewise religious education can never be equated with knowledge of religion, but entails as one of its aims a commitment to the practice of the truth of religious experience, a practice which includes a recognition of the importance of prayer and communal acts of worship.

Recognising the potential of the spiritual

Given that the proponents of religious education can demonstrate that the subject is not vulnerable to the above criticisms, religious education must still satisfactorily answer another challenge before its place on the curriculum can be justified: to what extent can religious education facilitate the realisation of recognised educational aims? In beginning to address this issue it may be worthwhile to reflect on one of the educational aims which receives prominence in the Green Paper and the *Report on the NEC* i.e. fostering an understanding and critical appreciation of spiritual values. From the point of view of the place of religion on the curriculum, one of the more striking features of the *Report on the NEC* is the recognition which it affords to the spiritual dimension of human nature. For example, Minister Bhreathnach's opening statement contains the following view which has been interpreted as signalling a need to redress the utilitarian bias of the philosophy of education in the Green Paper:

> But in facing these challenges (cultural, economic and demographic changes) we must recognise, value and affirm our cultural and spiritual heritage. If we fail to do this our education system will lose the characteristics which attune it to the Irish psyche and the Irish spirit.[32]

The *Report on the NEC* includes the following comment amongst its references to the importance of spiritual development:

> In short, educational policy and endeavour would be concerned to enable each pupil to appropriate from moral and spiritual tradition and from the plenitude of human learning, something of an abiding and sustaining sense of identity, amid the ubiquity of change in contemporary society.[33]

Interestingly, the recognition of the educational importance of fostering spiritual values is an integral part of the aims laid out in the Green Paper. It is twice mentioned during the course of the section entitled "Educational Aims," but, unfortunately, as with so much relating to values and ideals commonly associated with religious education, that is where it rests.[34] Even the most charitable reading of the Green Paper would not succeed in finding any sign that this educational aim has any discernible influence on the subsequent shape of the curriculum proposals. Although both the Minister and the *Report on the NEC* are concerned to reaffirm the validity of this aim (fostering spiritual values), one still awaits any sign as to how they would like to see it given effect in the shape of the curriculum. I suggest that the unpacking of this aim in terms of curriculum reform could provide a valuable contribution to redressing an over-emphasis on the enterprise culture and a valid way in which the state could give recognition to the value systems of the different religions. In saying this I am mindful that it is precisely the recognition of this educational potential of fostering the ideal of spiritual development which has given rise in the UK in the last few years to a concerted attempt to ensure that it is fostered at all levels of the curriculum.

What does it mean to speak of promoting spiritual values or promoting the spiritual development of the person? In an interesting article in the *British Journal of Educational Studies* entitled "Spiritual Development in the Education Reform Act"[35] Brian Hill argues for four distinctive marks of the spirit; endurance: referring to the continuity of self-identity through a person's life; transcendence: referring to such capacities as self-awareness and abstract reflection; creativity: referring to the capacity to exercise imagination and produce new permutations of ideas and materials; and dialogue: referring to the capacity to enter into relationships with other selves. His analysis provides a valuable pointer to some of the main features of what would commonly be regarded as belonging to the domain of the Spirit, even if his explanation of transcendence does not do justice to the experience of transcendence or the act of transcending whereby one reaches out beyond the strictly human to the one who is Other/Holy or God. However, notwithstanding the need for this corrective, the religious believer can without difficulty recognise in Hill's description of a spiritual person many of the qualities characteristic of a religious person. Equally important is the fact that by situating this set of human qualities within the strictly human he facilitates a recognition of their appropriateness as educational aims — even for those who may not fully share the religious convictions of convinced theists.

In terms of meeting the challenge to translate into practice the aim of fostering an understanding and critical appreciation of spiritual values, it would be beneficial to examine the approach which the educational authorities in the UK have adopted. In February of this year the UK schools inspectorate (OFSTED) produced a most interesting discussion paper entitled "Spiritual, Moral, Social and Cultural development"[36] which set out guidelines by which the spiritual, moral, social and cultural development aims might be translated into curriculum practice. While rightly careful not to equate religious education with any of these four aims, it nevertheless emphasises the relevance of religious education as a core subject for those whose concern is the fostering of these key educational aims. Interestingly, in its treatment of spiritual development it recognises that it is this spiritual dimension of human existence which allows each person the possibility of questioning the meaning of human existence, valuing a non-material dimension to life, and recognising the desire for an enduring reality. Spiritual development is therefore, as the document says, "concerned with questions which are at the heart and root of existence".[37] One of the most valuable aspects of this document is that it is concerned with the key question of how one effects a translation of these aims into the life of the school. Regarding the aim of fostering the spiritual development of the students the OFSTED document suggests four areas of school through which this might be realised: through the values and attitudes the school identifies, upholds and fosters; through the contribution made by the whole curriculum; through religious education, acts of collective worship and other assemblies; and though extracurricular activity, together with the general ethos and climate of the school. In terms of recognising the potential of the aim of spiritual development we could learn a lot from work done by statutory bodies such as OFSTED.

Conclusions: The dimensions of religious education

Anyone seeking to provide a rationale for the presence of religious education on the curriculum will inevitably focus on the importance of the educational aim of fostering the spiritual values which underpin human nature. Nevertheless an exclusive focus on this dimension of human existence cannot do justice to the scope of religious education. The following section which concludes this paper will endeavour to show why it is that educationalists have argued for a recognition of religious education as a core subject at all levels on the curriculum.

The first thing that must be noted is that it is only possible to value religious education if it is situated within a broader vision of a philosophy of education that is value/person-centred, a philosophy that both acknowledges ethical dimensions of human nature and recognises that students ought never be treated as means to an end. Furthermore, in contrast to the individualism and consumerism so evident in some educational philosophies and practices, it must be understood that it is only possible to understand and value religious education if one is conscious of both the interpersonal and teleological, or purposeful character of human nature. Finally, religious education presupposes that human beings, while free, are creatures marked by history and shaped by tradition — the living memory of the community. In this perspective, the history of religion is the history of the dialogue between faith and culture.

In the context of this vision the rationale for religious education emerges first and foremost from the singularly important dialogue between faith and culture. It is a dialogue which is informative because it recognises the way in which religion and culture are inescapably intertwined, particularly the way in which Christianity has shaped the history of European culture and has, in turn, been influenced by that culture. It is also a dialogue which is ecumenical — one that respects the values and beliefs of others precisely because it is sensitive to the way in which values and beliefs are appropriated in and through culture. Most importantly, it is a dialogue which is critical because it understands the prophetic role of religious faith and appreciates the contribution which religious faith makes to the important and necessary task of critiquing the dominant ideologies underpinning the prevailing culture.[38]

Secondly, the rationale for religious education is situated within the pedagogically recognised importance of promoting integration between the different elements of the school curriculum, as the following extract from the response to the Green Paper by the Episcopal Working Committee on Developments in Education points out:

> Religious Education plays a vital role in facilitating an integration of experiences in the humanities, sciences and in the practical subjects within the sensibility and character of the student. In religion class, the knowledge and understanding acquired in other subjects can be used to help young people to develop a holistic vision of life. Religious Education also provides a context in which some of the profound metaphysical and ethical questions implicit in other subjects can be addressed directly. Here we are thinking of the questions regarding humankind's nature and purpose which may be raised in teaching science; questions about the environment which may arise in teaching geography; questions about human moral responsibility which often arise in teaching literature, ... Indeed the teacher of religion may alert students to the moral stances which sometimes underlie such subjects as business studies or technology.[39]

Thirdly, an argument for the importance of religious education increasingly put forward by educationalists and government policy-makers, particularly in the UK, is its importance in providing an effective context for the development of moral values. The view is that despite the many positive benefits for society provided by the contemporary liberal culture, it nevertheless offers a very poor context for the development of a stable moral environment, because it encourages the viewpoint that moral values are relative and/or subjective.⁴⁰ This argument focuses both on the need for values to be grounded in a tradition if they are to be successfully imparted to succeeding generations, and also for the need to facilitate people, particularly the young, to find roots in a tradition.⁴¹ Whatever about this criticism of our contemporary liberal culture, it is certainly true that those who can identify with no tradition — those who do not belong to any discernible community — can find it difficult if not impossible, to appropriate a coherent set of moral values. Furthermore, it is undeniable that, in the context of our increasingly individualistic culture, the natural ties which root us in an identifiable community are less evident. Undoubtedly religion acts as a counterbalance to this characteristic of contemporary culture, and also has the capacity to provide a stable context within which the development of moral values can be fostered.⁴² What is probably most important is that, in giving recognition to an objective and transcendent dimension to ethics, religion testifies to a vision of morality which calls into question the emotivism which characterises much of what passes for moral reasoning in our contemporary liberal culture. In that context, religious education has unquestionably an important role to play in the development of moral values.

Finally, and most importantly, the rationale for the presence of religious education on the curriculum is situated in the context of a recognition of a dimension of human life that transcends the material. In particular, as the Mater Dei Institute's response to the Green Paper argues, religious education entails an acknowledgement of the validity of religious experience — understood as an intrinsic component of human experience and as the unthematised infrastructure of the various religious traditions.

> Such religious experience which exists as a universal possibility is grounded both (philosophically) in the common transcendent orientation of all humanity and (theologically) in God's self-communication in love to all humanity. ⁴³

Religious experience, expressed through the formulations of a particular tradition, is the primary subject matter of religious education. From there, its task is to compare and contrast the formulations of the same core of experience in other religious traditions. Such comparison and contrast would ensure that one's commitment to a particular tradition would be critical, and that one would be open to appreciate the rich diversity of religious experience as expressed through the formulations of the different religions.

There are many other points raised in these and other documents which suggest other perspectives within which the rationale for religious education on the school curriculum might be understood. Nevertheless, even within the confines of the four points mentioned, one can recognise that religious education, as so understood, could provide an important context within which many of the aims of education, as enunciated in the Green Paper, can be realised. In particular, it would seem that religious education has a significant contribution to make in the following areas mentioned in the paper.[44]

(a) Fostering an understanding and critical appreciation of the values — moral, spiritual, social and cultural — of the home and society generally;

(b) Promoting self-esteem and self-worth, combined with a respect for the rights and beliefs of others.

(c) Developing a spirit of inquiry and the capacity for the critical and constructive analysis of issues.

(d) Creating tolerant, caring and politically aware members of society.

(e) Creating an environment that is conducive to and supportive of emotional and physical well-being.

What is suggested by the above understanding of religious education is that, from a purely educational point of view, the failure to establish religion as a core subject at each level of the school curriculum would result in a significant impoverishment of the student's experience and would materially affect the student's capacity to interact creatively with his or her environment. It is without doubt a challenging scenario for educationalists to address.

50   Eoin G. Cassidy

Post-Script: Facilitating the development of the multi-denominational sector

In preparing for legislation which will determine the shape and place of religion in the schools for the foreseeable future, legislation which should enshrine the pluralist ideals of unity in diversity, tolerance and mutual respect, the peculiarities of the Irish educational system, both positive and negative, must be openly acknowledged. For various historical reasons, managerial control of the teacher-training colleges and the majority of the schools has up until the present been invested in the hands of the main religious denominations existing in the country. Given the high regard for religious belief which up until the present has characterised, and continues to characterise Irish society, the support given by Irish parents to this school system, and the high esteem in which Irish education is held internationally, one can certainly argue that this system has served and continues to serve Irish society well.

However, in the context of the cultural changes mentioned above and an increased awareness of the importance of the value of the ideals associated with pluralism, one must recognise that certain changes are needed — changes which respect the increasing evidence of religious pluralism and the evident desire among some parents for access to schools which are not run on denominational lines. In their submission to the NEC the Educate Together movement have put forward persuasive arguments which suggest that there is not at present a real and affordable opportunity for many parents who so desire it to have their children educated along multi-denominational lines.[45] Difficulties in respect of teacher training (the need for a college of education which would reflect the multi-denominational ethos), problems in acquiring suitable accommodation, and the uneven spread of the small number of these schools currently in existence, pose real problems for those seeking to respond to this demand. The detailed treatment of the issues raised by the Educate Together movement in the *Report on the NEC*[46] is evidence that the validity of their viewpoint is increasingly recognised.

It could be argued that the principle of fairness demands that multi-denominational and secular schools receive some special assistance to overcome these problems. Paradoxically, increased state support for the multi-denominational sector might be a welcome development for those who place value on the ethos offered by schools run on denominational religious lines. From their point of view, one of the more unsatisfactory aspects of the present system is that in terms of the educational wishes of some parents and teachers there is a *de facto* pluralism which is not, and cannot, be satisfactorily addressed in terms of the ethos of denominational education. This is particularly the case in regard to those parents and/or teachers who do not accept the validity of any theistic stand-point.[47] Given the absence of a sufficient number of multi-denominational and secular schools, the teachers in the Catholic and/or Church of Ireland schools are faced with the unenviable task of attempting to meet the demands of an increasing number of pupils whose parents, to a lesser or greater extent, do not share the values and/or beliefs which animate the life of the school. From the point of view of those who do not share the religious convictions of Christians, and who do not wish their children to receive an education in an environment influenced by Christian religious principles, the situation is equally unsatisfactory, particularly in the context of an integrated curriculum such as exists at the primary level. This unease with the present situation at primary level is evidenced by the increasing number of calls to separate the teaching of secular from non-secular subjects, a move which if agreed to would effectively mean the abandoning of the practice of integration. Given the almost universal welcome for the principle of an integrated curriculum at primary level, something echoed in both the Green Paper and the *Report on the NEC*[47] it would indeed be a pity if the integrated curriculum were to fall victim of a failure on the part of the Government to assist minority groups to set up their own school network. Finally, it must be noted that an increase in the number of multi-denominational and secular schools would assist those teachers who are ill at ease working in a denominational school to find employment in an environment which accords with their values and beliefs.

QUESTIONS AND DISCUSSION — SESSION ONE

CHAIR: Professor Áine Hyland

PANEL: Mr. Barney O'Reilly

Rev. Dr. Eoin Cassidy

Áine Hyland:
We now come to the first of the two discussion sessions in this symposium. Could I ask intending contributors to identify themselves before they speak, to keep their questions or observations to the issues covered by the two presentations we have just heard, and to indicate whether their comments are addressed to one or both of our panel members.

Paul Brennan (primary teacher):
While I found Mr. O'Reilly's paper very stimulating, I also found it wrong-headed; particularly in this sense. He spoke about education and schooling and did not once refer to the pupil as an individual. Now it seems to me that the educational process concerns the modification of the consciousness of the individual in a particular way and it happens ideally when a sophisticated intelligence comes into contact with a mind that needs to understand something. His references to Adam Smith and Karl Marx assume that the pupil is a social being, and of course this is true; but primarily the pupil is an individual. It is not the function of the school to impart ideologies, or indeed religions, or indeed any other overall view of human life. It is the function of the school to develop the individual consciousness: to ensure that the pupil learns not to accept simply what is fed to him or her, but to ask Why? Let me just focus on one particular aspect. The character of the Irish

educational system, since it was set up after the founding of the state in the early twenties, is a model of a propagandist vehicle. And the schools have connived with this, nowhere more so than with the church's view of social order, of the historical consciousness of what we are, and indeed the religious consciousness of what we are. All of this was based on myths; myths that were designed by various interest groups — the politicians, the so-called socio-economic theorists, and the church. The education system in this country over the years has kowtowed to these shibboleths. It has allowed itself to be misused. Fortunately, in recent years, we are coming to a position where education and educational philosophy is becoming independent of these things. It is now incumbent on us, whether as teachers, educational administrators, or theorists, but particularly as theorists, to ensure that education has an independent voice, that its concern is with the individual, that pupils are taught to question "why should we believe this?" I think neither of the two presentations tonight addressed this. The first speaker spoke of the educational system as an economic-social-political paradigm, and the second treated us to what I would see as a polemic on religion. The details of whether we should have denominational or non-denominational schools is neither here nor there in my view at a forum like this. What we need to address is the *why* of it, in the interests of the child.

Áine Hyland:
There are quite a few issues there. I think we'll take one or two more viewpoints from the floor and then ask the speakers here on the panel to comment.

Brendan O' Sullivan (teacher):
I also found Barney O' Reilly's presentation stimulating. I am not sure if he was suggesting that there should be indoctrination of economic or political ideology. What I find most interesting about the suggestions he made is that they provide us with a new context and a new framework within which to place considerations of moral education. And that framework can be found in the political development of democracy and the values for which democracy stands. For instance, liberty, tolerance and rationality, and indeed the promotion of autonomy. And I wonder if Dr. Cassidy would see a role for the cultivation in our schools of a moral character which is

specifically democratic; that is, a moral character which promotes rationality and autonomy, and one which recognises the necessity for democratic societies to agree on issues of right and justice, independently of comprehensive religious world views.

Áine Hyland:
Perhaps I would ask Dr. Cassidy to respond briefly to that and then bring in other speakers.

Eoin Cassidy:
Well, I am pleased to be able to respond to both speakers. With regard to the first speaker, he and I might be in more agreement than many people might presume. I think that education must be concerned with the individual. I am in agreement with him there. I also think that any true educationalist would abhor a propagandist model of education, and would be very critical of wherever this occurred. I think likewise that any talk or lecture that engages in polemics doesn't deserve much respect. And finally I do agree with him that the *why* of religion does need to be addressed. As regards the issue that the points I raised were polemical, well, I suppose one judges a paper on what one listens to. But certainly the focus of the paper was the *why* of religion. That was the focus, rightly or wrongly. There was a postscript, I will admit, on multi-denominational education, motivated in part by the presence of the chairperson here.[1] But that was a postscript. I think there's no point in going into a lengthy discussion on whether religious belief is based on myth, or superstition, or the like. A lot of people do accept your point of view. Clearly, as I said earlier, there is a division of opinion. Some people accept that religious belief is based on truth, others believe it's based on superstition. But one has to recognise one thing. And that is that contemporary educational literature, including the public documents issued here recently — including the 1992 Green Paper— do talk about developing and promoting spiritual values. Now when you begin to unpack that, it's very hard to ignore totally the dimension of human experience that we would call religious experience. It is very hard to ignore the way in which that has been formulated in and through the religious traditions. And if education is concerned with developing and promoting spiritual values, I think that many would argue that the teaching of denominational religious education is an integral part of that.

Now, just in brief response to the second speaker, I would agree with you thoroughly. I think that all schools should promote an education in rights, autonomy, democracy. I think it should be a compulsory element in all schools. All schools should show a sensitivity for instance to theories of human rights which form the basis of the various Conventions on human rights, including the UN Convention on the rights of the child and the European Convention on human rights. I think this should be part and parcel of schooling. Yes?

Brendan O' Sullivan:
But I am talking of rights outside of a particular religious view; in other words, an overriding priority of right, as distinct from a priority of a particular good.

Eoin Cassidy:
We're into a discussion here of the political philosophy of John Rawls, if I understand you correctly. Certainly Rawls' arguments for a priority of right over a priority of good would be one of the leading components of a theory of justice in a liberal society. There are others who would disagree with him; for instance, an equally eminent philosopher such as Alasdair MacIntyre, who takes quite a different view. That's one which many people have argued at length on. My position has more in common with the viewpoint proposed by MacIntyre than that proposed by Rawls.

Áine Hyland:
There's someone else over here keen to get in, Yes?

Fergus Keegan (primary teacher):
I enjoyed both speakers and would like to thank them. Mr. O' Reilly was talking about mono-integration as being unhelpful. Well, I advocate that the parish network system of schooling in Ireland cannot be bettered, and that it has proved its worth over a long time. And I don't think that there is any viewpoint otherwise to suggest any dismantling of that system. And if anything, it (the present denominational primary school system) is a blocking vehicle to what I would call rampant secularism. The other side of the coin is the question of interdenominational and separate schools — and I've

never heard as good a case for them before as Dr. Cassidy's. I welcome that, because if the voice is there seeking such schools, they should be set up. And I think in the past, church suspicions and state obstructions have not helped those schools. Thank you.

Áine Hyland:
Would anyone else like to contribute now? While we are waiting for further contributions from the floor, I'll call on Barney O' Reilly to respond to the points that have been put to him so far.

Barney O' Reilly:
In response to Mr. Brennan, I accept the criticism you offer that I was not focusing on the individual, or the centrality of the pupil in the educational process. To that extent, my presentation could have been viewed as unbalanced. But I was attempting to redress what I perceive to be an imbalance in philosophical discourse on education, and part of my thesis was that too much of the philosophy of education is focused on the role of education in relation to the individual, without much reference to what you acknowledge yourself as the social dimension. And I was focusing on this dimension, particularly its political and economic aspects. I am not at all suggesting — and I would be very unhappy with the suggestion — that an educational system, or the processes of education, should be totally subservient to the economy or the political system. I would have the same objections that you would have to an education system being manipulated in that overriding way. Unlike you, however, I would contend that there is a real and legitimate function that school systems perform in both economic and political life. I was attempting to direct the concerns of philosophers to those, as areas that I think are important in tackling our current educational dilemmas. Now in response to Fergus Keegan's point about the parish network, can I just offer you this reflection for consideration. Inherent in the concept of the parish network as the basis for schooling is a concept of community which is linked intrinsically to church organisation. Perfectly valid. But it's not the only concept of community that's out there. I would go so far as to suggest that in the context of our larger social and political difficulties, the almost exclusive link which is established between the community — as church community — and the schooling system

dysfunctional in our society, particularly in view of the current historical dilemmas we are in.

Áine Hyland:
There's another speaker at the back

Donal Leader (Marino Institute of Education):
I've just been reflecting on both papers and I see both in terms of a question which is probably the background question for much of the discussion here tonight. It has been implicit in a lot of what has been said already. My question concerns the nature of democratic society itself. It seems to me that one of the disjunctions in various proposals about the nature of democratic society is in fact the public/private disjunction, or what is presented often as a disjunction. In Barney's paper the focus was very much on the public world— seeing education very much in terms of economics and politics. And to some extent, Dr. Cassidy's paper was about the defense of certain values and orientations in the private world. It seems to me that this whole debate about religion in society and religion in education concerns whether religion fundamentally has to do with the private world or the public world. In democratic societies there is a very strong resistance to seeing religion as having anything to do with the public world, much less the political world. And so you get this very strong reluctance on the part of democratic societies to see public monies going to support what is essentially regarded as the private domain. I am wondering in particular if Dr. Cassidy saw his argument as going any way towards defending the political role of religion, if indeed it has a political or public role.

Áine Hyland:
Thank you Dr. Leader. There is one more person trying to get in.

Anne Colgan (National Parents' Council):
This is a question mainly for Barney O' Reilly. I wasn't entirely clear whether Barney was suggesting that there was a valid distinction between a philosophy of education and a philosophy of schooling, but he seemed to use the terms interchangeably throughout his paper. And I would like to ask him to comment on my contention that the absence

of that distinction in both our philosophising about education and in our policy-making has very negative consequences. Consider, for instance, the great amount of informal adult education that goes on outside of the schooling system. This must be considered part of the education system, but all too often its not. What would the import of your arguments be for this field of activity? If we concern ourselves with schooling to the neglect of education, moreover, there is a danger that this will result in playing down the need for linkages and managed transitions between all the learning contexts in a child's life, in playing down the right of communities to be involved in the governance of schools, and perhaps most especially, in placing an inordinate burden on schools to be both the vehicle of change and the vehicle of conservation.

Áine Hyland:
In a philosophical debate, it is only after some reflection that things really begin to move, but unfortunately, time is also closing in on us now. Of course we have another discussion tomorrow, but before we finish tonight's session I will give each of our speakers an opportunity to reply to the questions that have been put to them: Eoin Cassidy to Donal Leader's question and Barney O'Reilly to Anne Colgan's.

Eoin Cassidy:
Thank you for the point you raised regarding the private versus public character of religious belief. There's no doubt about it that in contemporary society there is a move, if one might use the phrase, to "privatise" religious belief. But anything which attempts to deny the political character of the religious dimension of human life distorts religious belief. The political character of human life is an integral part of human nature. We are not just private individuals. We are political, social beings. Religious experience is a dimension of the whole person. Consequently, it necessarily impinges on the political and social aspects of human life. I would agree with you that the attempt to suggest that religious belief is in some way not relevant to public life certainly distorts religious belief.

Barney O'Reilly:
There is a real dilemma for me in Anne Colgan's probing observations. I made a very explicit statement early on in my paper that I was equating — for the purposes of this debate — the philosophy of education with that of schooling. My thesis sought to link the organisation of schooling as we know it— for instance pupils in class groups and the institutional formats of schooling — with the emergence of other major social phenomena which I identified: Firstly, the identification of the economic system as a reality and the attempt to study it formally, and secondly, the rise of democracy and nation states. I saw a deep-seated linkage between those two phenomena and the rise of schooling. Your observations have pointed out a difficulty with my thesis, in that there is in an education system more than what we understand by a schooling system. And I think I would have to acknowledge that my paper doesn't attempt to take account of those dimensions of an education system which you very rightly drew attention to. I don't think that invalidates however what I had to say about schooling systems, which are the dominant mode in which education is delivered and experienced. But I do think that the paper would need some reworking to take into account the dimensions you have drawn attention to. Thank you. (See also note 7 on O'Reilly's paper above. Editor).

Áine Hyland:
On behalf of the Educational Studies Association I would like to thank our two speakers for getting us off to a fine start tonight, and also to thank all of you who have contributed to the debate. Your contributions have helped us to reflect on, and perhaps to rethink, many of our assumptions. Tomorrow promises to be a further challenging and interesting day, with three papers: from Dr. Joe Dunne, Dr. Kevin Williams and Dr. Pádraig Hogan. Go raibh maith agaibh go léir, slán abhaile agus oíche mhaith.

NOTE
1. Professor Hyland is President of "Educate Together," the national movement for multidenominational schooling in the Republic of Ireland.

What's The Good of Education?

Joseph Dunne

Introduction

It is encouraging, in the role in which we have been asked to speak here, that many of the responses to the Green Paper, *Education for a Changing World,* lamented the absence from it of any coherently articulated philosophy and that the opening chapter of the *Report on the National Education Convention* affirms that "the provision of an adequate philosophical rationale ... remains a priority."[1] In an age when there tends to be a specialised provider of every service, it would be a neat division of labour if philosophers could be called on for the provision of this "rationale" — if their expertise could be relied on to sort out otherwise bedevilling, vague, or contentious issues of values, fundamental assumptions, and overall aims. It would be no compliment to philosophy, and no service to education, however, if these bothersome issues were assigned to it only in order to clear the ground for an unencumbered consideration of all the other, apparently more tractable and "real" considerations: strategic planning, efficient management, adequate resourcing, effective delivery, and so on. The first task of philosophy, indeed, is to question any such convenient separation of ends and means or of value issues and technical ones. For while this separation allows an advertence to aims or values to be granted a privileged status at the beginning of official documents this can all too easily turn out to be the dubious privilege of a purely aspirational, not to say ceremonial role; they may not then be seen as carrying any implications for, or as having any power to penetrate, the functional or technical issues which are addressed in the subsequent discussion.

In this preliminary marking out of the ground, I will offer an interpretive comment on the two major documents we have had so far, the Green Paper and the Convention Report, as well as on the debate which occurred in the interval between them. Thus I may find an opening into a more satisfactory philosophical engagement with this debate. It was a notable feature of the Green Paper that in a quite bold and vigorous way it inserted education within a wider matrix, especially an economic and social one. The overall sense of its message to educators was: the school is not a cultural oasis; the environments and worlds that we live in and that schools willy nilly are part of, are changing rapidly and inexorably — so that in our understanding and practice of education we must situate it realistically within some wider sense of where this social and economic change is taking us and what it will require of our pupils if they are to negotiate it in ways satisfactory and enhancing to themselves and to society.

Now much of the critical response to the Green Paper sprang from a belief that its understanding of the broad context was in fact too narrow — that its concern with the economy and the labour market occluded other, more humanistic, concerns (especially spiritual and artistic ones). Or, put somewhat differently, that the Green Paper's too partisan and unreserved espousal of a productivity-driven society and its "enterprise culture" seemed to want to harness education *in the service* of this society and culture rather than to see it as, in some respects at least, in unavoidable conflict with it. Critical responses to the Green Paper from many diverse sources, then, were motivated by a sense that in some strands of its thinking it had *colonising* ambitions towards education (casually betrayed in its language — most conspicuously perhaps in its renaming a school principal as "chief executive" — but also in its restriction of the wider community to be represented on school boards to the business community); and that it therefore needed to be resisted in defence of the autonomy or, perhaps better, the *integrity* of education.

If this was the thrust of a great deal of the response to the Green Paper it seems to me that the later Convention Report reflects it in a particular way: in a certain withdrawal from the wider arena of discussion and a more focused preoccupation with education as a distinct and autonomous sphere. Curiously, however, this intramural move does not seem to lead to a very close focus on what is really specific or proper to education; a great deal of the discussion is about issues such as administration, management, planning, control, accountability, and quality assurance. These issues do, of course, come into play in important ways in education and there is no reason why they should not feature in discussions and reports. They are not, however, unique to education — a fact which is evidenced by the curiously content-neutral language (now in very wide currency) which they seem to attract. Moreover, there is a danger that preoccupation with them can replace attention to fundamental issues about the identity of education — without which they themselves cannot be adequately approached.

These fundamental issues do not mainly arise in intramural reflection, and if we want to defend the integrity of education we can do so only by first acknowledging how deeply and perplexingly it is challenged, not primarily by the economist ideology which forms a definite strand of thinking in the Green Paper, but rather by the reality of the kind of society in which we live and must try to educate (and of which the Green Paper happens to take an up-beat view). If, as so many people have said, a philosophical dimension has been signally missing from the debate, this is mainly because we have not given sufficiently close and vigilant attention to the real predicaments that face educators in an advanced industrial, or, increasingly, post-industrial, society such as our own. The philosophical task as I see it — and of course it is a task for all of us and not just for philosophers — begins with a recognition of just how deeply problematic education is in our society. In what follows I try to analyse the nature of these problems and to articulate an approach that may be helpful in grappling with them.

The Burdens of Contemporary Schooling

In one sense schools are curiously sequestered zones, with their spatial aloofness from the workaday and domestic environments, their routine exclusion of "outsiders," their suspension of the ordinary rhythms of experience, their adherence to a strict timetable, their paraphernalia of uniforms and other rituals that lend them a strange continuity with an ancient academy, not to say a mediaeval monastery. And yet, of course, despite the almost timeless icon of the schoolhouse, or the archetypal images of teacher and pupils, our schools have very vulnerable borders with the "outside world." To be sure, they still, as ever, introduce children to the basic literacies, to competencies in the notational and symbolic systems of the society, and beyond that initiate them in some systematic way into disciplines of knowledge. On these tasks the school has a pretty exclusive franchise and they still seem to define its proper and inalienable function. And yet, clearly, to focus only on this function is to neglect the complexity of the school's role in a modern society.

Consider first, then, the way the school is asked to carry the burden of what society still officially considers sacred — even though it may not be prepared to do much or suffer much on its behalf — other than to project responsibility for it onto the schools; I am thinking here of Irish (the Irish language) and of religion (mainly the Catholic religion). Or consider, next, issues which surely are experienced in society as very real; increasing crime and delinquency, drug abuse and various other forms of abuse that reveal large cracks in the civic, and familial, fabric. When these problems are discussed is it not again the school which is so often looked to as the source of a solution — if, that is, it is not seen as itself a cause of the problem ("there's no discipline anymore in schools")? Or consider, then, those less malign issues that periodically come on the agenda of social concern. There is the environment and issues to do with pollution, conservation and the promotion of a green consciousness and lifestyle. Or new senses of how oppressions have been rife — though often largely unrecognised — and can no longer be tolerated. Issues of gender equity come to mind here but also development issues, new senses of global interdependencies and of the responsibilities of the richer countries of the North to the poorer ones of the South. Or the stronger awareness of the need for ways of tackling prejudice and dealing with difference, that has found expression in e.g. programmes of anti-racism, conflict-resolution and peace studies. Or, again, an awareness of the power of the media in our lives which has given rise to media studies (or computers, and computer studies). Or, finally (though the list could go on), a new awareness not exactly of sex, I suppose, but of the importance as well as the dangers associated with sexuality in contemporary society, that has prompted calls for more adequate programmes of sex education. Take all these together and you have a big bundle of priorities accumulating at the school door, with claims for entry being made on behalf of all of them — and meanwhile with the exit door firmly closed on anything that might be dismissed in order to accommodate them. But that is not all. Consider next the imperatives laid on the school by the state. Any state must expect its schools to perform a strong socialising function — to equip young people with kinds of knowledge, skill and conviction that will fit them for citizenship as it is defined in that state. For a democratic state one might expect that the crucial requirement of schools would be that they educate young people in those civic virtues (such as a deliberative concern for the public good, a sense of tolerance and of social responsibility) without which the more external marks of democracy become empty forms. In fact, however, democratic states do not always seem to put a premium on principled education for citizenship: In Ireland, the fate of civics, as well as of various efforts to establish a coherent programme of social and political education, illustrates this neglect. It is a very different function that schools take on as their primary role in advanced industrial democracies — and perhaps nowhere with such extreme efficiency as in Ireland. They take on the function of social selection, of assigning people, on the basis of their performance on (usually centralised) examinations, to the various occupational slots — with corresponding levels of income and status — that are available in the society. Education thus becomes the primary means whereby individuals can promote their self-interest, their private economic gain. The democratic state's concern with this transaction is to increase the fairness of the playing pitch on which it is conducted; hence, the prominence in the Green Paper of issues to do with equity.

Education, Production and the Economy

We come close here to what is perhaps most problematic for a modern educational system: the extent to which it is implicated in the functioning of the economy. This fact imposes an instrumental role on education which (though many lament it) may be essential and not merely accidental to a *modern* education system. A brief historical advertence will help to bring this fact into focus. Our most venerable picture of a non-instrumental type of education, one that would be pursued simply for its own sake, comes to us from Greece. A salient fact about ancient Athens, however, is that it was not a democracy. In a sense, of course, it was the birthplace of democracy, giving us not only the name but the ideal of this form of politics. But it was not a democracy in a sense which we could now accept, quite simply because of its drastic restriction on the range of citizenship; only a small fraction of the adult population were citizens. This elite, among its other privileges, could benefit from a liberal education — but only because all the work of production and reproduction was done by the disenfranchised majority, which included slaves, skilled craftsmen and women. If we now aspire not only to universal suffrage but to mass education this is surely because our egalitarian conscience is more developed than was that of the Greeks. But this aspiration would have remained just that — an aspiration — if something else had not intervened, namely, a huge shift in the nature of knowledge and of its role in society. This shift has really only occurred in the last century, indeed with decisive influence in Ireland only in the past few decades.

A great extension of the democratic ideal and a big move towards some sense of universal rights was certainly ushered in by the eighteenth century Enlightenment; and yet when Thomas Jefferson, who was quintessentially an Enlightenment man and one of the founders of the new American Republic, founded the University of Virginia he was unabashed in asserting that its doors should be open only to "a handful of geniuses." If we now regard this as unacceptable this is not necessarily because we espouse egalitarian values more strongly than Jefferson did; what makes the crucial difference is the fact that now, far more than then, knowledge has actually become (what Bacon, nearly two hundred years before Jefferson, had already anticipated) power — ultimately the power to produce and transform. It is primarily this change in the role of knowledge that underlies the huge change in the scope of access to education. So long as knowledge stood apart from production, no society could afford to have more than a small minority devoted to the pursuit of knowledge through education; for it needed as many hands to the wheel as it could muster. And if by contrast our society tries to provide something like universal education, this is not because it is any less concerned than earlier societies with the imperatives of production; it is simply that the productive person now is the educated person. The realisation of this fact in Ireland was most conspicuously evidenced in the title of perhaps the single most influential policy document in the history of Irish education, *Investment in Education*.[2] The relationship between education and the economy has become a reciprocal one, with dependency running in both directions. On the one hand, the productiveness of the economy depends on the educational system for the supply of a skilled workforce (what is increasingly called "human capital"). On the other hand, the educational system depends on a productive economy for funding on the scale which is required by a modern democratic system of schooling — even one as relatively under-resourced as our own. This interlocking of education with the productive and economic sphere circumscribes the autonomy of education, rendering problematic the ideal of a humanistic education without utilitarian purpose. For if schools were to break the tie in one direction by defining an agenda of their own which was not, at least in some important respects, responsible to the needs of production, they would themselves be casualties of the tie broken from the other direction; because of their ceasing to feed the goose there would no longer be the golden egg which feeds themselves.

The Points System

A major consequence of the phenomenon I have just been analysing presents itself in the most concrete and real way in every student's experience and every parent's or ordinary citizen's perception of education nowadays. Its most manifest presentation is in the competitive Leaving Certificate examination and the points system based on it. This system dominates the consciousness of students, the work of teachers, and the attitudes of parents in post-primary schools. It determines entry to third level education of every kind. And it has even exerted an influence downward on primary schools in the pressure which has been felt in the senior classes to succeed in entrance examinations to secondary schools. It is the focus of huge media attention twice yearly, as a great public ritual is enacted of pre-exam speculation and prediction turning, paper by paper, to post-exam analysis and debriefing — and all of this to be succeeded a few months later by the appearance of results and the labyrinthine process of assigning, through the exact and impassive medium of numbers, a whole generation of young adults their most tangible life-chances. If this is the most public — one might say the most blatant — aspect of Irish education, one cannot conclude from the Green Paper or the Convention Report that it is very significant. In her opening address to the Convention, the chairperson, Professor Donnelly, said to the assembled delegates: "It is not only what you are aware of which is interesting, but what you have forgotten." These words of the chairperson's might be taken to invite a deconstructive reading of the Report, with attention not so much on what is said in the text as on what is not said — what is absent or "forgotten." If the forgotten participants of the Convention were the pupils (who remained absent, while so many other "partners" — at least forty different groups or representative interests altogether — were present) perhaps the forgotten issue, not only in the Convention Report but more seminally, and less understandably, in the Green Paper, is the points system. In the section on assessment in the latter, it is only testing in the primary school and evaluation of the new Junior Certificate that merit attention,[3] while the single most obtrusive — and, I want to argue, most problematic — feature of our whole educational system is passed over in silence.

The points system is the most clear-cut line at which education meets up with the socio-economic system. Through Leaving Certificate results this wider system uses the education system to select people for progression towards the various job opportunities that it makes available: the progression in the first instance for an increasing proportion of students is into and through third level education and the different courses which, with varying degrees of specificity, provide more immediate access to these occupational slots. There are very large questions to be asked about the rationality of this selection mechanism from the viewpoint of the partner which it most clearly serves, i.e. employers. It is rational to the degree that those selected for different occupational pathways are indeed more suitable for these occupations than others who desire them but who are excluded. And this will be the case if exam performance is indeed a good indicator of potential accomplishment for the job (or in other words a good predictor of future actual accomplishment) so that we correctly infer that proficiency in exams will translate into adeptness on the job. There must be large questions about this — when many hugely heterogeneous types of slot use the one same instrument of selection, and no attempt is made, through specific tailoring of different tests, to ensure in each case a strong correlation between what is tested and what is required on the job. There are questions here which are important for the overall effectiveness of our society as well as for the happiness of many persons within it — not only those who fail on this basis to find any employment but also perhaps many others who succeed only in finding work that is less congenial than they might otherwise have found. But I shall not follow out these questions here. I propose rather to look at another question, or set of questions, which arise at the same contact point, but which focus on the effects of this arrangement not on the socio-economic system, but rather on the other partner, namely education. What are the effects on education of the fact that *it* is now the decisive agency in determining people's economic futures?

The fact that the selection process occurs only when post-primary schooling is already completed does not prevent it from having a huge effect on the nature and significance of school experience itself. The most obvious effect is that by greatly raising the stakes in education, for many students (and their parents) it solves at a stroke the whole problem of *motivation*. It supercharges the significance of one's school performance, now cashed out in terms of exam results, making it almost redundant to ask, why study? why work? why bother? For a significant number of other students, of course, it may open a gaping motivational hole: why bother when it is already so clear that in *this* race one is an also-ran. The question that arises here is whether or not the effect of all this is beneficial to education. What this arrangement adds, from the viewpoint of education, is a set of extrinsic rewards. This addition does nothing to enhance the quality of education, however, unless it alters *in a positive way* the students' relation to what I want to call the *intrinsic* goods of education. In fact what is all too likely to happen is that these external rewards, precisely because they are so powerful, rather than acting as helpful incentives, can subvert or displace the intrinsic goods by becoming themselves the end; and then education has in a sense gained the world, but in doing so, has lost its own soul.

Education and Equity

To judge whether or not this is in fact now the case in Irish education, we need to understand what these intrinsic goods of education are — or, in other words, to have a tolerably clear and defensible answer to the fundamental question posed in the title of my paper, "what's the good of education?" I want to go on to suggest an approach to answering this question. But before doing so, let me clarify matters here by indicating a few points which I am *not* committed to arguing. I am not suggesting that there should be no evaluation or assessment of educational achievement. And though I would argue that a great deal of emphasis in education should be on self-evaluation, i.e. on helping the learner to assess her own progress — *as part of the learning process* — I am not rejecting in principle any system of assessment by others, inside or outside the school, at the end of post-primary schooling. Neither do I deny the need for a rational system of selecting people for available opportunities in work and in third level education — a need that is clearly more acute when there are significantly fewer opportunities than there are aspiring candidates. Indeed, given that these two processes — of educational assessment and of social selection — have come to coincide so much, and notwithstanding the fact that I have just been pointing out problems that stem from the way they coincide at present, I see great difficulty in arguing that, without radical changes in our socio-economic structures, they should be decoupled.

For, in our existing society, it is easy to imagine undesirable consequences of such a decoupling. If school attainment were no longer to function as a determinant of a person's chances on the job market then it would be replaced in this function by something else. Different employers as well as third level institutions, for instance, might devise their own entry tests. In that case, however, schools would be under enormous pressure to incorporate preparation for these tests (or at least for those of them on which success was highly prized) into their own agenda — alongside their now more restrictively defined educational work. If schools were to succumb to this pressure the problem which the restriction had been intended to solve would now have simply reappeared in a new guise. But, even if schools were successfully to resist this pressure, a different and surely undesirable consequence would be likely to follow: preparation for these tests would devolve on to the market, with "academies" of various kinds springing up to cater for it. It is one of the less desirable aspects of the points system that it has already spawned a plethora of these institutions — increasingly, in recent years, not just as adjuncts to, but as replacements for school. But if the work of schools were to be marginalised in the selection process these entirely private institutions, conferring huge advantage on those who could afford to attend them, would be at a far greater premium. And, in terms of social equity, such a development is unconscionable.

It is already a huge challenge to our society to bring about greater economic and social justice and in particular to break the cycle of poverty which tends to perpetuate disadvantage from one generation to the next. Any commitment by the state to meet this challenge could hardly set aside the educational system in which the state itself already has a huge financial stake. There are already very formidable barriers to realising the ideal of "equality of educational opportunity" even within the state sector — and quite apart from the growth of private enterprise in the field of general education. Many of these barriers are deeply entrenched in existing class structures and social patterns that make it extraordinarily difficult for schools on their own to exert much leverage on them. Hence, the depressing evidence that even when schooling has replaced more traditional mechanisms as the dominant agency of social selection, it confirms the biases of these earlier mechanisms: children from poorer families still tend to do less well in school and to remain poorer themselves as adults.[4] Despite all this, however, schooling policy, in tandem with other socio-economic policy, needs to address the problem of educational "underachievement" due to disadvantage; and in this regard it might be said that one of the more commendable features of the Green Paper is its emphasis on equity. The point I make here, though, is that equity in education can hardly be divorced from a fuller economic and cultural equity throughout society. And, if this is so, it is hard to see how educational assessment and social selection could be entirely sundered from each other.

Equity may be granted to be a necessary corollary of any ultimately defensible education; but it still remains a formal concept insofar as it concerns the *distribution* of goods — where the latter can be characterised and vindicated as goods, however, only by invoking some other, substantive sense of "good," which is not contained in the notion of equity itself. And here a more radical perspective might be introduced into our analysis. For it could be argued that the whole constellation of rewards, in terms of jobs, status and income, which is on offer through the points system, and the distribution of which is the focus of conventional discussions of "equity," is itself gravely deficient in the "good." This is the case because of the undesirable nature of the work enshrined in many existing jobs, in terms either of social impact or of import for the individuals who do it, for example, dehumanising, boring and repetitive, lack of autonomy, or low wages, and because the number of "jobs" is, in any case, perhaps inevitably, declining as changes in technology make it possible to create more wealth with less work. More generally, it is the case because of the dubiousness of "taken-for-granted aspirations, reward criteria and understandings of success and happiness ... (as well as of) the existing rules by which status, wealth and power are allocated."[5] The claim here might be that the established social structure is becoming increasingly dysfunctional even with respect to the dynamics of its own material base. But the more substantial claim is the moral-political one that it is indefensible, irrespective of which individuals slot into which positions within it, in terms of any serious concept of justice; and hence that a concern to render equitable the basis for selecting people for differential slots within it, (i.e. the mechanism through which it is perpetuated), is ultimately incoherent — at least if "equity" is to remain tied to a strong concept of justice and not just to a very "thin" sense of "fairness."

Even if one inclines (as I do) to this more radical analysis, one must still acknowledge that it is the present system, deeply entrenched, and pervasive in its effects, that individuals involved in education — pupils, their parents, and their teachers — must now contend with. And it is hard to argue that, individually, they ought to act as if it did not exist — or that, so long as it does, it is not preferable that an admittedly limited and compromised ideal of "equity" should not be pursued. For the work done in many jobs *is* socially valuable as well as personally rewarding and, moreover, many of the things that can be acquired only through money are also substantive goods or at least necessary conditions for the enjoyment of substantive goods (only a particular kind of saint or mystic could, without hypocrisy, deny this).[6] It is hard to expect, then, that if access to these goods is tied to opportunities that depend on educational success, albeit within a stratification that is not systematically justifiable, this fact will not greatly influence attitudes to education itself. Despite this, however, I still want to argue that these opportunities are, and should be recognised to be, *external* to education. I say they are external because I take it that a person might enjoy them and still not be an educated person; while, conversely, a person without them, or with them only to a very limited degree, might be a truly educated person. But if this is so it invites once more our fundamental question, which surely requires fuller analysis: what is the educated person, or what are the goods *internal* to education?

"Internal Goods" and "Practices"

The form of this question should not suggest that it is amenable to an essentialist answer, or that an ahistorical analysis will yield an idea of education, valid beyond every cultural development and difference. Still, I shall try to articulate a set of concepts that may be firm enough to give some coherence and justification to the endeavours of "educators" — while being open enough to comprehend, or at least not in principle to exclude, the density and variability of the concrete conditions in which "education" has to be brought to life. First of all, what I'm calling an internal good arises only in the context of a practice that a person becomes engaged in. A practice is a coherent and invariably quite complex set of activities and tasks that has evolved cooperatively and cumulatively over time. It is alive in the community who are its insiders, (that is to say, its genuine practitioners), and it stays alive only so long as they sustain a commitment to creatively develop and extend it — sometimes by shifts which at the time may seem dramatic and even subversive. Central to any such practice are standards of excellence, themselves subject to development and redefinition, which demand responsibleness from those who are, or are trying to become, practitioners. We may look at this relationship to standards of excellence in the characteristic activities and tasks of a practice as a submission that imposes a discipline; but it is also, of course, this discipline which enables or empowers people, in a very real sense of that sometimes abused or, at least, overused word. For through real engagement with, and in, a practice a person's powers are released, directed and enlarged. The denotative range of "practice" in this sense may be illustrated by examples as various as cabinet-making, physics, farming, chess, computer-programming, metal-work, history, rearing a family, music-making, drama-production, soccer, weaving.[7]

Engagement in the characteristic tasks of a practice, which embody standards that challenge one insofar as they are beyond one, leads, when it goes well, to the development not only of competencies specific to that practice but also of moral qualities that transcend it — that characterise one not just as a practitioner in that domain but as a person in life. To really engage with a practice in the sense of striving to realise the goods intrinsic to it — and not just to treat the practice as a means for attaining external goods (external in that they might equally be achieved by other routes, e.g. money, status, reputation) — is to acquire, in doing so, qualities such as honesty and humility (in admitting the shortcomings of one's attempts), as well as patience and courage in sticking at a task, even when it does not offer immediate gratification, and a sense of justice and generosity in cooperating with others in projects that require a kind of partnership which overrides the rivalries of individuals precisely insofar as it responds to the demands of the practice itself. And a thing worth noticing about what might be called the economy of a practice — when we stay on the inside of it — is that it is not an economy of scarcity. In other words, if one person really comes to excel, this need not be at the cost of other people's chances to develop *their* talents. Every achievement of excellence enriches all who participate in or care about a practice; it can be an occasion for admiration or even celebration as well as sometimes, of course, for attempts at emulation.

The case is otherwise when we look to the *external* goods or rewards which can attach to success in the practice. When it comes to distributing *these* goods, whether they be money or jobs, especially in a society that finds it increasingly difficult to create jobs, there is scarcity, everyone cannot be a winner. And this remains the case even if we make great progress in terms of equity *in education.* Extending educational provision — when at the same time real job opportunities remain severely limited — clearly does not increase the number of winners. At most what it achieves, when our focus now is on external rewards, is, firstly, inflation of the educational currency, (so that

Leaving Certificate becomes equivalent to what an Intermediate Certificate was a decade or two earlier, or what a primary degree will be a decade or two later); and, secondly, not more equality but rather inequality with a different base, a stratified society still, but stratified now on the basis of scholastic achievement, or attainment in exams. To be sure, this basis may be less questionable in a modern democracy than the earlier basis of (unmediated) family background and inheritance; but it is still a basis for inequality of a type which is itself very questionable.

The notion of an internal good, and its distinction from an external good, may need some further clarification — if only to forestall any impression that practices are closed, esoteric spheres, accessible and of benefit only to specialists or professionals. In the first place, competencies and virtues acquired and exercised by practitioners are not the only internal goods of practices; also to be included among the latter are more objective achievements, e.g. a well-made cabinet, wholesome food, a melodious tune, increased knowledge of the past of a local area of community, or a well-designed experiment — which are internal goods of the practices of cabinet-making, farming, music-making, history and chemistry, respectively. Secondly, to say that a broadly conceived good is internal to a practice which has become professionalised is not to imply that the professionals have any exclusive competence, let alone concern, with respect to the achievement of that good. At the level of a very general characterisation, health, for example, is a good internal to the practice of medicine; but it does not follow from this that the role of the doctor (or nurse or other "health care professional"), or the institution of the hospital, has any monopoly in the enterprise of protecting or improving health. (And, *mutatis mutandis*, the same of course is true with respect of education, teachers and schools).

Thirdly, there are important practices which, even though they contain possibilities of great virtuosity, are nonetheless available with real integrity at quite modest, even rudimentary, levels of accomplishment. Examples of such practices are writing, reading or playing a musical instrument. It seems likely that many people have been greatly short-changed in their education, precisely because they were introduced to these activities not as practices, but rather as sites where decomposed drills, exercises and "micro-skills" were rehearsed as means, while a taste of the whole activity as an end was continually deferred or displaced. There are approaches, however, through which small children can come to experience these activities in their wholeness; they then participate in them in a way which is personally meaningful to themselves — and in which, incidentally, the continuity between their engagement and that of "great masters" (a very heterogeneous grouping) is very real.[8] Fourthly, there is a sense (and this, incidentally, was the original sense)[9] in which the concept, "practice," designates a whole area of activity which is precisely non-specialist in that no one can be excluded from participation in it. The practice I speak of is the practice of living, more especially living as a member of a community (or increasingly, of several distinct communities) and as a citizen of the polity. Here, "good" takes on its widest and most contestable connotations, and its realisation calls for capacities of deliberation and judgement and for the exercise of moral and civic virtues. Education in more particular practices should, I believe, contribute to the cultivation of these capacities and virtues. but perhaps the most significant contribution of schooling in this respect — positively or negatively — lies in the "hidden curriculum" or ethos of the school, the ways in which it constructs the role of "pupil" with respect to issues of authority, responsibility, and decision-making.

"Practices" and Education

Having introduced the notion of a "practice" and having attempted to forestall some possible misgivings about it, I shall now try to outline more positively the kind of help it may offer in understanding education. I have stressed standards and also the difficulty — and, because of the difficulty, the discipline — involved in responding to them and thus becoming a practitioner. This may seem an over-austere view which, if taken up in education, would be at odds with our current concerns that children be happy, well-adjusted and, perhaps above all, have high self-esteem. It needs to be pointed out, though, that the discipline involved in real learning is not a suppression of desire. For the desire of the person must be awakened and drawn out, and, as it were, drawn in by the goods that the practice has to offer — so that one comes to care about these goods and even to love them. This is true of a child learning to play chess, make things with wood, play football. There are indeed restrictions in all of these; castles just can't be moved diagonally, a nail hammered only in a particular way will go in straight, and only if one's foot, eye and whole body are finely disposed in balance, coordination and timing can one dribble, cross, or volley. But these restrictions can be accepted for the sake of the immense, almost limitless possibilities that are opened up by chess, woodwork or football as practices. These possibilities can come to lure the learner, to attract and as it were to captivate him — so that he willingly, even joyfully, submits to the demands that they make.[10] And it is in giving himself to the pursuit of structured possibilities of this kind, embodied in practices, that he finds himself. For it is his own powers that are extended through his pursuit and realisation of the possibilities offered by the practice. And this is a way to a real, deeply grounded "self-esteem."

In extending this analysis of a practice to a consideration of education, it may be noted that in its range of application, "practice" is inclusive. In itself, it provides no basis for discriminating between "cognitive" and "practical" (or "manual") domains — let alone for privileging one above the other. And so, in making this the core concept in our understanding of education, we give no hostages to the kind of "academic" bias which traditionally has dominated curricular policy in schools — a bias which may be particularly acute in a country like Ireland which, for historical reasons, lacks strong traditions in the crafts and trades, but which in any case goes back to the Greek philosophers and has been powerfully reinforced in the modern era by the baleful influence of Descartes's wholly distorting split between mind and body. Young people can surely be educated through engagement with a practice such as woodwork, metalwork or music-making, when such an engagement involves the following: release from the tyranny of the ego through a focusing and concentration of energies on goods that transcend themselves (thereby paradoxically enabling them to discover and realise themselves); release from a vacant present through partnership in a tradition that is richly alive in the present, stretches back into the past and, partially through them, can be extended forward into the future; the achievement of competencies which are ones of the whole person and which, just because they are rooted in the body, do not for that reason call any less into play qualities of creative insight, judgement and expression, which only a terribly limited cognitive psychology could fail to recognise as qualities of *intelligence*. In looking at education into a practice in some such way as this I would also, of course, want to see it as being *in itself* in a very strong sense a *moral education* insofar as, properly conducted, it involves, as I have already suggested, the learning not only of skills but also of virtues.

There is one other point here: the competencies learned, as I have stressed, are enabling ones and therefore give a kind of resourcefulness and *mastery*. This is important, but genuine education into a practice will also develop qualities of appreciation and *receptivity*. The whole frame of modern culture — inscribed most deeply in the project of exploiting technically the resources of modern science — has tended to be one of control, mastery and domination. The intended domination has been of the earth and its resources in the first place but more and more of our own living, too. It is becoming ever clearer, however, that this aspiration to technocratic control does not have within it the wisdom to bring about conditions that make our social and personal lives more just or fulfilling; to the contrary, in its unidimensional approach to finding solutions, it often relocates, adds to, or even creates, the problems. This has not prevented it, however, from offering to our culture a beguiling and deeply influential ideal-image or hero-type: the expert (invariably male) who is invulnerably in charge, who can set his goals confidently and manage things, other people, and even himself, effectively in order to deliver success. Such a type seems to provide the ideal of the educated person in important sections of the Green Paper; in the chapter on "Broadening Education," under the heading, "Educating for Life," the first aim for students is: "An ability to manage oneself and to make the most use of personal resources."[11] It is clear from the language here that a deeply technocratic and instrumental orientation has been imported into the attitude to oneself that education is to promote. And the point I wish to make here is that the educational value of "practical" subjects would be greatly diminished if they were to succumb to this technicist ideal; and that an important element in their being genuinely educative is that they should open students to a sense of admiration, and sometimes even of awe, at the possibilities and also, of course, the historical achievements in a practice.[12]

It would be a mistake to suppose that the "practical" subjects are the only beneficiaries if the notion of practice is made central to our conception of education — by being rescued from the prejudice which has relegated them to second class status. For the more traditionally valued academic subjects benefit at least as much — if only by being extricated from the superficial understanding of their supposed virtues which was the obverse side of the condescending attitude to "practical" subjects. The sort of things that I have said about "practical" subjects should be true also of "academic" subjects such as history, physics, English literature or biology. In each case it is an ongoing practice that students need to be introduced to — a practice that embodies its own ways of conducting inquiry, asking fruitful questions, imagining or empathising with characters or situations, devising plausible hypotheses or interesting interpretations, sifting and weighing evidence, making creative connections or shifts of perspective, identifying and reflecting on basic assumptions, becoming sensitive to different contexts, making critical judgements. All these (and much more besides) involve activities that are specifically patterned in each practice, though clearly there are common or overarching types of activity that allow one to speak in the general terms I have just used. It is these activities, with the criteria and standards built into them, that students need to learn. Apart from them, facts, concepts, or propositions make no sense; and only through them — discussion and cooperation with others — can students be enabled to think and thereby to come into the full exercise of their own minds.

Teaching and learning in the light of Practices

While I do not claim that the notion of a practice can by itself answer all significant questions about education, it does carry some strong implications for the conduct of teaching and learning which are worth a brief elaboration. Emphasising practices would combat the tendency which seems to be deeply endemic to schooling in almost all cultures towards a "recitative script," with the expectation that teachers will "instruct and assess" and that pupils will "absorb and regurgitate." Instead, the expectation would be that teachers are practitioners in different domains who find ways of introducing pupils to the practices, and inviting them to become themselves practitioners at the level of proficiency to which at each stage they can aspire.[13] Pupils would be involved in activities and tasks, and in the conversations and discourses that arise in attempting to perform them. Teaching/learning would involve a strong element of apprenticeship in that students would *do* history or *do* physics and the teacher, as well as arranging opportunities for this to happen, would provide significant modelling of what in each case it entails. These activities, with the materials, texts and tools that go with them, would provide a medium between teacher and pupils in relation to which each could be agents (cognitively as well as in other respects).

It is through participation in conversations that arise in the context of focused tasks that people truly develop their repertoires of thinking, feeling, speaking and acting as well as reading and writing. Creating contexts that elicit and sustain such conversations is the great challenge to schools. And the great art for teachers is to be responsible not only to the opportunities and demands of the specific practice but also to the needs, aptitudes, and difficulties of particular pupils.[14] It is the latter requirement that makes them teachers, that is to say people competent not only in the specific practices that give substance to education, but also in the peculiar practice that is *teaching itself*. This double requirement gives a paradoxical character to what is perhaps the essential interaction in educative teaching, namely, "instructional conversation." "Instruction" and "conversation" appear contrary, the one implying authority and planning, the other equality and responsiveness. The task of teaching is to resolve this paradox. To most truly teach, one must converse; to truly converse is to teach.[15]

For pupils, the fact that they are recipients of instruction through being at the same time participants in conversation, and apprentice practitioners, gives an integrating character to their learning. Insofar as they are drawn actively into the open texture of a practice they more readily take what Howard Gardner calls "risks for understanding" rather than relying on "correct answer compromises."[16] And in this mode of learning their newly acquired knowledge is not only integrated by the structure of the practice itself (which in some cases, e.g. in mathematics or in physics, can reach rarefied levels of abstraction); it is also integrated into their own developing cognitive/emotional structures. And this latter fact acts against one of the most limiting aspects of much school learning, its frozenness in one compartment of the mind, so that it does not interact with other areas of schooled knowledge, let alone illuminate aspects of non-school experience. This is one of the great difficulties of teaching:

how to enable students to "bridge" between the "official" knowledge of the school and their own informal, personal or "life-world" knowledge so that the latter is enriched and challenged by the former.[17] For students are hardly educated unless what they learn in school penetrates their ways of thinking and feeling and informs their reading not only of books but also of their own experiences and worlds.

Stressing the need for "schooled knowledge" to animate and inform out-of-school experience is not reducible to a point which resounds in the Green Paper, echoing comments on education from other sectors: that schools should take their cue, so to speak, from the existing or emerging society and bend their efforts to serving its needs. The point I wish to make, rather, is that education should indeed equip people to address their present society — and of course the shape of their own lives within this society — but that it will not adequately do this unless it enables them to reflect critically on this society by offering them fuller perspectives on the human good than they find instantiated in its institutions and practices. The life and death of Socrates, perhaps the first exemplary teacher in our Western tradition, is testimony to this point. Anything less might be an education of consumers and even of producers, but not of citizens

Conclusion

In concluding the paper, I am aware that there are important issues, implicitly raised by my own analysis, which I have not addressed. Here are a few: What historical forces shape the emergence — and decline — of practices? What criteria should govern the selection of some practices for inclusion in the content of education — and the exclusion of others? By whom, and through what process, are these criteria themselves to be determined? In what respects will these criteria differ for pupils from different places and backgrounds or of different ranges of age and aptitude? How could existing school subjects be reconceived as "practices" and how hospitable would the latter be to curricular integration or to interdisciplinary initiatives? Would an emphasis on practices bring into relief radical alternatives to existing "subjects?" How substantial a reorganisation, indeed redefinition of school would be necessary in order to accommodate practices as the central endeavours of the institution? and, very crucially (as the point at which internal goods are most vulnerable to external pressures), what modes of assessment are most congruent with the characteristic fabric of practices?

While I have not attempted to answer these questions, I hope that I have provided a conceptual context which gives them point and pertinence as questions. The answer I have attempted to sketch to the wider question posed in the title of the paper is not intended to offer anything like a blueprint that might then be systematically implemented; practices cannot be established through the medium of a technicist logic. It is largely for this reason that, over a long period, many successive waves of "school reform" in many countries have come unstuck. Without a willingness to enter the core reality of a practice, they have sought, in "top-down" fashion, to specify "outcomes" and have conceived the task of effective management as one of getting teachers to maximise these outcomes and making them accountable for doing so. It is a hopeful sign that the ineffectiveness of such a model of change and the need for alternatives to it is now more widely recognised (conspicuously, indeed, in the Convention Report); and that this recognition is accompanied by a greater appreciation not only of the difficulty of changing schools but also of the great need to do so.[18]

So long as we entrust huge responsibility for education to schools, any adequate approach to educational reform needs to ensure that these are learning institutions for all who are involved in them — teachers, administrators, and parents, as well as pupils. Nothing I have said implies that education should be conceived as the narrow preserve of specialists; clearly, it is too important to every citizen for this ever to be the case. At the same time, it follows from the stress I have put on practices that teachers, as the practitioners who are most centrally engaged in education, are the ones on whom the achievement of its goods most heavily depends; and it follows from this that their good as practitioners should be a paramount consideration in all educational decision-making. This good is not well provided for when teachers are permanently isolated in their own classrooms as "deliverers" of a prescribed curriculum. Perhaps their greatest need is proper opportunities for the kind of focused conversation about their own activities as teachers that they, at their best, make available to their pupils in their learning activities. There are hopeful signs that, despite the contrary pressures, spaces for such "conversations" have been growing in recent years (in this respect the National Education Convention itself was a welcome initiative). It is only from such conversations, rooted in and faithful to the texture of educative practice, that reform in assessment procedures as well as in modes of school organisation can come. The burden of my paper has been not so much to suggest ways of bringing about such reform, as to sketch a conception of the internal goods of education which might help us to identify what is to count as genuine reform. If educators do not attend vigilantly to these goods there is no shortage of other functions that will be pressed upon them. When they do attend to them, education acquits itself as education *and* best serves the wider society — even if there is much in this society to block a proper recognition of this fact.[19]

Philosophy and Curriculum Policy

Kevin Williams

"There are more things, in heaven and earth, Horatio, than are dreamt of in your philosophy."[1] When Hamlet makes this observation to Horatio he is using the term "philosophy" to refer to Horatio's beliefs about the world. In ordinary English when we speak of someone's "philosophy," we too are referring to the beliefs which inform that person's life or to the rationale behind particular patterns of action. While it is perfectly acceptable, if slightly inflated, to speak of an individual's "philosophy," I am not persuaded that there is much to be gained in attributing to society's system of organised learning a "philosophy of education." Indeed, odd as it may appear from a lecturer in philosophy of education, I prefer to avoid the term altogether and simply speak of values and priorities in education. One reason for wishing to avoid the expression "a philosophy of education" is due to its association with high faluting utterances about the "plenitude of human personhood" and the "fullness of human understanding" which no one could possibly disagree with. Another reason is that those who aspire to the definition of a "philosophy of education" sometimes seem to assume that this philosophy will produce a consensus on educational values. We can have a consensus on clichés but the aspiration to define educational values capable of securing universal approval is unrealistic.

Why is it that we cannot expect to achieve consensus on educational values? There are at least two reasons. In the first place, if values are to engage universal assent they have to be expressed in so general a form as to be almost meaningless. For example, in her John Marcus O'Sullivan lecture, the Minister for Education proposes that society should aim to provide all young people with "every opportunity for personal development in order to fulfil their potential" so that they "will emerge from the system as rounded persons."[2] No one would possibly disagree, but as a practical proposal it does not amount to much. The problem is not with the values aspired to but rather with how these values are to be interpreted. This applies to most of the words in the quotation — "every opportunity," "personal development," "rounded persons." For example, if we try to unpack the term "rounded persons," we shall discover that people differ greatly in what they are prepared to count as "rounded persons." In the second place, many values of a humanitarian nature, such as concern for others and consideration of their interests, willingness to share and to co-operate, are also problematic. Those whose world view is theistic would find them incomplete. Others, some parents and maybe even perhaps some school authorities, would find them inimical to the robust individualism ("entrepreneurship" to use the current jargon) which they would like to see fostered in children.

Philosophy and Education

It is not surprising that philosophy cannot generate consensus. This is because philosophy as a discipline or form of inquiry is agnostic about the ends of human life and is impotent to yield universally compelling conclusions about the "good life" or human well-being. Philosophy is not the avenue to some arcane insights known only to, and shared by, its practitioners. If philosophy were the route to shared insights, then we could expect some consensus of opinion on the great metaphysical, moral and political questions. Let me illustrate this by reference to the famous debate about the existence of God between Bertrand Russell and Fr. Frederick Copleston. Listeners to the debate, which was broadcast on radio, must have been surprised at the profoundly intractable character of the disagreement between the two men.[3] Their shared commitment to the methods of professional philosophy led to no meeting of minds on the fundamental questions which divided them. Likewise, in the unglamorous sub-set of the discipline occupied by philosophy of education, disagreement with regard to substantive positions among practitioners is endemic. Among philosophers of education we find

Marxists, socialists and free marketeers, liberals, conservatives, theists, secularists, advocates of culture-centred, society-centred and child-centred theories, and, of course, individuals who advocate different shades and combinations of these viewpoints. Their views are as varied as those of the practitioners of any other of the educational disciplines or, indeed, of any interested non-philosopher citizen. Although they work in the same discipline, philosophers of education have different views or maybe even different conceptions (Marxist, liberal, conservative, Christian, Islamic, secularist) of education. It is, I argue, less confusing to use the term "philosophy of education" to refer to an academic discipline which is concerned with constructing and appraising the plausibility of arguments rather than to affirmations of particular attitudes on educational issues.

This should not lead us to conclude that philosophy has little contribution to make in helping us come to grips with substantive issues in education. Determining the persuasiveness of different viewpoints is a matter of philosophical argument. We might expect (although, alas, it is not always so) that the arguments of philosophers will be more cogent, learned and rigorous than those from outside the discipline. But argument on central issues in philosophy of education will always be informed by the orientation of our fundamental moral values and perhaps even of our personalities. I believe that there is a sense in which deeply-held convictions about major issues in education derive from realms of the human personality which we can penetrate only with difficulty. Consider, for example, arguments about the use of corporal punishment or the policy of compulsory Irish, or even about schools' policy on the wearing of uniforms. There comes a point on certain issues where we reach a bedrock of value beyond which argument cannot carry us. Here we say: "this is what I believe to be essential for human flourishing and well-being and we would be in dereliction of our duty to the young generation if we failed to do our utmost to pass on these values and beliefs." In this respect our attitude is like Luther's — "here I stand, I cannot do otherwise."

This does not mean that everything is a matter of contention — and that there can be consensus on nothing beyond clichés. But this consensus is not easily achieved. For example, we might agree that young people should be taught to be literate and numerate and to acquire basic historical and geographical knowledge. Yet, even here problems may arise. Those who recall the arguments about revisionism in Irish history will realise that the definition of appropriate historical, and even, geographical knowledge is problematic. Nonetheless, it is wise not to problematise everything and it is important not to introduce false dichotomies into educational discourse. I am thinking, for example, of discussion in Ireland about the relation between liberal education and education of a more practical nature. Today there is a fairly sharp polarisation between "liberal educators" and "trainers" whereby advocates of opposing views tend to see one another in uncomplimentary terms as "Luddite traditionalists" or "Philistines of fashion." This is part of a regrettable tendency within education to see everything in stark either/or terms.

There can even be some meeting of minds with regard to education in values. For example, there is a close relationship between the values which are promoted in schools hospitable to a Christian religious ethos and moral values in general.[4] Many of the central moral values promoted in such schools are also acceptable to many non-believers. Generosity, concern for others and consideration of their interests, willingness to share and to co-operate, courage and steadfastness are among the values which inform a religious ethos and which would be perfectly acceptable to believer and non-believer alike. The moral vision of Christianity, moreover, is expressed in compelling images and metaphors. Think of the story of Adam and Eve, the Tower of Babel, of the injunctions in the Sermon on the Mount or of the parables. The ideals of human conduct enshrined in such parables as the Good Samaritan and the Prodigal Son form part of the moral capital of Western civilisation. In our century, the lives of such Christians as Maximilian Kolbe and Mother Teresa are capable of providing exemplary moral inspiration.

But here I wish to enter two notes of caution. In the first place, where there is a consensus, this does not mean that it should be accepted uncritically. For example, in Ireland for many years now there has been an almost universally shared consensus that schools should be used to engineer a new political loyalty by promoting the notion of "European citizenship." Government documents, such as the Green Paper of 1992, enthusiastically contribute to this consensus. Although the authors of responses to the Green Paper disagree on many issues, most take the opportunity to deliver themselves of some exhortations endorsing the promotion of the "New Europe." But support for the valuable elements in the European dimension of civic education does not entail support for a contrived notion of citizenship for inhabitants of nations who have long civic traditions of their own. Moreover, educators can articulate the interdependence of nations and of peoples and thereby facilitate all kinds of transactions between them without recourse to the kind of extravagant proselytism which was used to create nation-states in the past.[5]

In the second place, education is not simply a matter of putting an icing of different values on the same cake: different values produce a significantly different cake.[6] Our educational values are not addenda to a separate, neutral set of values which we can comfortably share with others. Our values are woven into the stuff of how we conceive of human life and its purposes. And this conception of human life will inform the kind of education which we seek for our children. This point has implications for the controversial issue of the integration of religion with other subjects in the primary curriculum.

In a sense, some level of integration between school subjects is inevitable.[7] As long as a school provides religious education, religion is bound to have some influence on the treatment of other subjects, both at primary and at secondary levels. (Here I am talking of religious education rather than the kind of study of religious beliefs which is best described as sociology of religion). As religion touches on everything that is significant in human life, issues with religious implications arise in the teaching of many subjects at primary and secondary level. For example, questions regarding humankind's nature and purpose arise in teaching science and questions about human moral responsibility often arise in teaching literature. It is not easy to see how a pupil could avoid the influence of religious education without opting out of the culture of the school. Indeed, religious sensibility is expressed in the Irish language itself in such idioms as *Dia Dhuit and Beannacht Dé ort* (similar to Grüss Gott used in parts of the German-speaking world) which communicate something of the theocentric quality of the Irish way of life. Obviously it would be impossible to teach Irish without teaching these theologically-imbued expressions.

So where does this leave us with regard to the role of philosophy in education? What philosophy can do is to help us to attend critically to the plausibility of arguments about education. The critical role attributed to philosophy must not be confused with the uttering of standard generalities which purport to "critique" the "inequities" of the "system." The critical role which the philosopher assumes is rather different. In this role, the philosopher acts as underlabourer whose job it is, as John Locke puts it, to clear "ground a little" by removing "some of the rubbish that lies in the way to knowledge."[8] Locke's concern is that:

> (v)ague and insignificant forms of speech, and abuse of language, have so long passed for mysteries of science; and hard and misapplied words, with little or no meaning, have, by prescription, such a right to be mistaken for deep learning and height of speculation, that it will not be easy to persuade either those who speak or those who hear them that they are but the covers of ignorance, and hindrance of true knowledge.[9]

Locke's characterisation of the task, indeed of the duty, of the philosopher is one which has always commended itself to me. This task is to introduce clarity into discourse, expose inconsistencies and unexamined assumptions, draw distinctions, detect fallacies and irrelevance in argument and generally show up jargon, clichés and other nonsense for what they really are. Locke's prescriptions (he was, after all, a medical doctor) would prove therapeutic for writers on educational issues. These prescriptions would provide a particularly salutary astringent to those who write in the current idiom of educational fashion. It is a pity that Locke's wise counsel is not heeded by those who, for example, like to represent the curriculum as a "quality managed product" which is "delivered" by "reflective practitioners" under the direction of "co-ordinators of learning resources" in the "rapidly changing technological society" which is our "post-modernist world."

To attribute to philosophy a role as guardian of careful argument and plain prose is not to deny it a constructive role.[10] For example, *Education and Meaning: Philosophy in Practice,* a recent exciting book by Paddy Walsh, an Irish philosopher living in Britain, shows how it is possible to respect demands for rigour in argument while constructing the kind of comprehensive grand theory which was eschewed by the conceptual technicians in the analytic tradition. I wonder if it is significant that books on philosophy of education by Irish authors tend to have this wide compass and address educational issues from a holistic perspective. This applies to Donal Mulcahy's seminal *Curriculum and Policy in Irish Post-Primary Education as well as to Autonomy and Schooling* by Eamonn Callan, to the fine studies of the educational thought of Martin Buber and Tolstoy by Daniel Murphy, to Joe Dunne's magisterial work, *Back to the Rough Ground: Phronesis and Techné in Modern Philosophy and in Aristotle* and to the forthcoming volume by Pádraig Hogan.[11] On a more modest scale, this essay attempts to make a fairly extended argument about the school curriculum in Ireland. In the first place, I try to show how the discipline of philosophical thinking can help us to get clear about fundamental issues in curriculum policy. My second aim is to show that, although it cannot tell us what we can and should teach, philosophy can inform our reflections on these matters.

Philosophy and the School Curriculum

It is one thing to claim that the philosopher can help us to understand useful (and even not so useful) distinctions, it is quite another to show how it does so. Firstly let me attempt to show how philosophy helped me to get clear about the focus of this essay. It was through making a distinction between experience, education, schooling and the curriculum. Experience refers to all that befalls us and education refers to all that which has been designed for the purpose of teaching us something. Schooling refers to the normal context within which the education of young people is conducted and the curriculum refers to prescribed, learnable activities which are normally amenable to assessment. It is important to bear in mind that schools are not the only institutions which provide education. Education takes place within the family and community and at times through the media. Within schools, the formal curriculum is not the only instrument of education. Education occurs through participation in a school's culture and a school's ethos is the expression of this culture. Although the curriculum is not all there is to teaching and learning, the focus of this essay is on this central, but also tangible, specifiable aspect of education. I wish to focus attention in this way, otherwise, in seeking to talk about everything, we can end up saying nothing.

When we turn to the curriculum itself, philosophy can also help us to make distinctions between the different human practices (skills and forms of understanding) which we might include within the curriculum. A clear map of its conceptual geography is a prerequisite of coherent thinking about the curriculum. How then might we distinguish between the different areas which seek inclusion within the curriculum? The following sketch aims to make clear some central distinctions:

1. Traditional subjects:
   (a) The Humanities;
   (b) Mathematics and the Sciences;

2. The Practical and Arts/Crafts Area;

3. Direct Personal and Social Education including Preparation for Work. Personal and Social Education has two aspects:
   (a) Informative;
   (b) Formative.

The essence of the formative aspect of Personal and Social Education is the development of communicative competence, the character of which shall be explored later in this essay.[12]

An Outline of the Argument

The main part of this essay consists in a philosophical consideration of the current post-primary curriculum. Firstly, I attempt to show how philosophy can clarify the necessary and limiting conditions and assumptions which underpin the design of the school curriculum. The first condition concerns the limited resources which the human race has at its disposal in implementing even its most admirable of projects. The second condition concerns the necessary and crucial role which assessment must play in respect of all teaching and learning.

The next part of the essay includes an examination of the value and limitations of the traditional concern of the school curriculum with the written word, i.e., literate and numerate culture, especially at second level. Particular attention is devoted to what I consider to be the most conspicuous failures of the conventional curriculum in terms of promoting the benefits of learning.

The School Curriculum: Necessary and Limiting Conditions

Firstly, let us consider what is a limiting condition of any school curriculum, namely, the issue of resources.

The Issue of Resources

Human beings live in servitude to the scarce resources of their world and these resources include time. The school curriculum is not elastic and not everything which we might consider useful or worthwhile can be included within it. There are only twenty-four hours in a day and we cannot hope to ensure that young people will learn at school everything which we think would be of value to them. Therefore we need to establish priorities with regard to curriculum design. For example, the trend of curricular policy in Ireland (and in the United Kingdom) is to make the study of a foreign language compulsory in schools. But what degree of priority should be conferred upon foreign languages? Should they have precedence over Irish, over geography/environmental studies, history, civic/political studies, science or technology/practical subjects? If we decide to add any new requirements, we must ask whether it is to be at the expense of existing curriculum areas. If not, then where is the extra time to be found and how are the extra resources and personnel to be provided? In introducing new curriculum areas, we have to ask questions about resources. Where, for example, are the resources to come from to provide the Leaving Certificate Vocational Programme or the Leaving Certificate Applied Programme to all those who wish to take these courses? Aspirational rhetoric is a pleasant indulgence but curriculum policy also needs the astringent of realism.

Resource allocation is a matter of choice on the part of those who administer the educational system. But the issue of choice also arises for pupils. Perhaps the issue of resources would be somewhat less acute if it was decided to reconsider the extent to which we wish to prescribe areas for compulsory study. In this respect it might be fruitful to specify the extent to which the choices of young people are to be taken into account, if at all. For example, is it wise that Irish should be the only compulsory subject on the standard Leaving Certificate course? Anecdotal evidence suggests that at least some pupils would not choose to study the language at senior cycle if they were given a choice.[13] Does this matter? If not, why not? On the issue of pupils' freedom to choose in respect of Irish or of any other subject, the philosopher can simply point out to policy-makers areas where justification should be provided and invite them to provide it.

Obviously there is much more to be said about the issues which I have just raised which cannot be pursued within the context of a single article. But let us now turn to an important necessary condition of all learning, namely, assessment.

Assessment and the Curriculum

If human beings want to learn anything, from learning to tie their shoe laces to learning to solve problems in nuclear physics, then it is inevitable that they will want to know how well they have been doing at what they have been learning. For this reason it can be said to be a matter of logic that notions of assessment/examination and degrees of success/failure are associated with all learning.[14] Assessment is not therefore an optional extra in learning but is rather a necessary, integral feature of every human effort to acquire mastery of a skill or body of knowledge. It is important to stress this because otherwise assessment can be perceived as an external encroachment on what would be otherwise an enthusiastic, spontaneous and free activity of learning. Questions may well be raised about the manner of assessment in certain circumstances but the idea of assessment itself cannot be dispensed with.

The reason for this is that human activities have criteria or standards of success built into them. These criteria or standards have nothing directly to do with the personal qualities of the learners, although such qualities as diligence and perseverance are likely to contribute to success in learning. In determining the criteria of success at such activities as swimming or mathematics, willingness to try hard and other positive personal qualities, however admirable, are not relevant. We might, for example, wish to applaud a student's interest in the German language and willingness to do his or her best to learn it, but if the same student fails to understand or to make the simplest utterance in the language, then we have to say s/he has been an unsuccessful student of German. But failure to meet the criteria in our performances at particular activities does not mean that we have failed as human beings. Failure to master the German language, to learn to swim, or to play a musical instrument does not diminish our value as persons. All it means is that we lack ability in certain spheres of human activity.

Sometimes too it is important to know how we are doing in relation to other learners. This does not mean that we are intrinsically competitive but rather that in many spheres of learning it is necessary to have an idea of what the norm of achievement is within the activities in question. Someone learning to swim all on her own, without any idea of what others can do, may acquire an exaggerated notion of her ability merely because she is able to swim one width of the pool. There is then nothing inherently objectionable in the notion of norms and they have nothing to do with Darwinian notions of sorting people into hierarchies of worth to the community. Again it must be stressed that the failure to reach even the minimal norms of achievement in such activities as swimming, speaking German, or playing musical instruments does not make us inferior to those who attain the highest levels of accomplishment in these areas. It means only that others are more competent than we are at certain human activities. It is seriously misguided to attribute the relative lack of success of individuals at certain activities to a conspiracy on the part of a socio-economic elite to contrive criteria and norms which prevent the poor from achieving success at them. Economic factors play an important role in determining the distribution of many of the benefits of education but these factors do not define the criteria of success or the norms of achievement within educational practices.

And it may well happen that we have ambitions in certain areas but that we lack the abilities to realise these ambitions. Unfortunately it can happen that our ambitions can exceed our abilities. Individuals may wish to be great soccer players, great violinists, great actors, great historians, great physicists or great physicians but may be unable to meet even minimal standards or criteria of performance in the areas in which they wish to succeed. Or they may have only the slightest of talent in relation to the standards attained by others in these spheres. Assessment is required to give us an indication of the relationship between our abilities and our ambitions in the relevant areas. And it is only sensible and appropriate that people be given an idea of the relationship between their abilities and ambitions. The fact that our ambitions can exceed our abilities is an unfortunate reality of life which it would be foolish to deny. It applies in most spheres — individuals may have ambitions in sport, the arts, in scholarship or in the professions, but they may simply lack the ability to realise these ambitions. This means only that they lack certain abilities; it does not mean that their worth as human beings has been diminished. Let us next turn to a consideration of the value and limitations of the conventional curriculum.

The Conventional Curriculum

With the rise of industrialisation, organised learning in schools and colleges became vital in supporting the system of industrial production. Moreover, in most jobs literacy and numeracy were an advantage and often a necessity and this was one of the factors which led to the introduction of mass schooling. As society came to demand many diverse skills, the school became the arena where the first stage of initiation into these skills took place. It is important to realise that formal education or schooling has traditionally been concerned with learning of an essentially intellectual or cognitive nature. This is communicated in the use of the term academic to refer to much of the learning carried on in schools. Academic learning is learning which is based on the written word and on abstract thinking. It is the learning which is peculiar to the academy, that is, to an institution which is a place apart from the "getting and spending" of everyday living.[15]

Formal education in our society is centrally concerned with academic abilities, that is, with cognitive, intellectual or theoretical abilities — or with what we might call abstract thinking. Let us then consider the character of this thinking a little more closely. In the normal conduct of our lives thought is required. It is required when we have to think about what we should or might do. Should I walk, or take the bus, or should I take the car? In this kind of situation we have to consider the advantages and disadvantages of different courses of action and, in the light of this reflection, decide what to do. Thought, in the sense of taking care and paying attention, is also required in the doing of whatever we decide to do. As we are driving our car, painting the front door or tuning the television set, we are thinking in this sense. Thinking in these senses might be called concrete, engaged, or embedded thinking because it is rooted, engaged, or embedded in particular practical or concrete situations of real life.[16] Abstract thought, on the other hand, deals with situations in terms of the general principles involved. If someone writes a letter to the paper advocating the banning of private motor cars from the city centre, this thinking is abstract rather than concrete. The thinking is disengaged from the particular, once-off, concrete decision as to whether or not to take one's car today. This shows that activity of a theoretical character does not necessarily entail work within the academic disciplines. Any systematic enquiry requires theorising — from deciding whether to bring one's car into town to deciding whether to marry a particular person.

Now the traditional concern of the school has been with the thinking represented by the established academic disciplines. The thinking conducted within these disciplines is of immense practical value. Without the abstract thinking of our mathematicians, scientists and engineers we would enjoy few of the very practical and concrete benefits which a technological civilisation offers us. The academic skills which characterise abstract thinking are therefore crucial to our civilisation. The skills of mathematical and linguistic reasoning are not just optional accomplishments within our culture: they have become an essential feature of it. The academic skills of analysing, explaining, synthesising, interpreting, weighing evidence and attending to nuances of meaning are vital human accomplishments. For this reason we must be wary of the fashionable tendency, at least at the level of rhetoric, to make us feel guilty about valuing academic ability. We must not measure human worth in terms of such ability but such ability cannot simply be dismissed as "bookish theory" or "mere prattle without practice."[17]

The kind of thinking which has traditionally been the concern of formal schooling does not come at all easily. Let us pause a moment to consider why this is so. In terms of the history of the human race the kind of abstract thought which we have developed is relatively new. After all, literacy has been widespread only since the introduction of compulsory schooling in the last century. Therefore, the academic skills based on abstract thinking and on mastery of written language are not only comparatively new to the human race but they are also somewhat at odds with the way most human beings would tend to function naturally. Human beings take delight in physical activity and have an ability for thought which is perfectly adequate to deal with the practical, concrete situations of everyday life. But abstract thinking based on the written word requires a special kind of discipline and effort which explains why it does not necessarily come easily to us. And it is this kind of thought and the discipline which it requires that schools are concerned with. It is then no wonder that Shakespeare, long before the introduction of universal compulsory schooling, spoke of the schoolboy as going unwillingly to school. And even such a giant of Western civilisation as Saint Jerome complained of the ardours of intellectual labour.[18] It is therefore perhaps because abstract thinking is so hard that our society attaches such value to success in the areas of abstract thought.

But it is important not to be simplistic or naive about the need for academic ability in certain spheres of human endeavour, for example, in such occupations as teaching or medicine. A student who fails pass mathematics in the Leaving Certificate is unlikely to become a successful maths teacher, or someone who fails pass biology is unlikely to become a successful medical doctor. An important reason for there being such an emphasis on achievement in the academic sphere is due to the esteem attached to academic/professional work in this society. We may regret that parents and pupils should have such narrow notions of esteem and that the competition to gain access to courses in such areas as law or medicine is so intense. But the notions of esteem held by so many and the competitiveness which they give rise to are not the concern of this essay and I shall spare the reader any platitudes on the matter.

At this point I wish to comment on what has historically been the most persistent criticism of the conventional curriculum, namely, that its primary concern is with the "product" rather than the "process" of learning. This seems to be a confused and unhelpful criticism and I shall try to explain why.

Product, Process and the Conventional Curriculum

In educational discourse, the precise meaning of the "process/product" distinction is not always clear. Indeed, such philosophers of education as John Kleinig, Robin Barrow and especially David Carr raise doubts on the plausibility of the distinction when used with regard to learning/assessment.[19] (These are doubts which I share and which I have explored in detail elsewhere).[20] My suspicion is that part of the tendency to make much of this questionable distinction derives from the misguided tendency to associate intelligence with prior cognition ("process") rather than with action ("product"). One lesson which Ryle has taught us is that the presence of prior reasoning is not relevant to our characterisation of an action as an exercise of human intelligence.[21] This is because it would be impossible ever to act intelligently if an exercise of intelligence had first to be prefaced by an intellectual operation. If a prior intellectual operation is necessary to make an action an exercise of intelligence, we still need an explanation of what makes the intellectual operation itself intelligent. If we invoke a further prior mental act, then we find ourselves in an infinite regress. As the intelligence of an action cannot be located in a prior intellectual operation, its intelligence has to be elucidated in terms of the context in which it takes place. Furthermore, the identification of intelligence with reasoning would make it self-contradictory to speak of "stupid reasoning" and, of course, this is not self-contradictory. It is actions themselves rather than their putative antecedent ("processes") which express human intelligence. There is perhaps an irony in this use of a classic argument from Ryle in order to cast doubt on the distinction between "process" and "product," as the distinction itself may well derive from other distinctions made by Ryle— the celebrated task/achievement distinction and the distinction between "knowing how" and "knowing that."[22] Let us turn now to a closer analysis of the use of the "product/process" distinction in the educational context.

In brief, it might be said that "product" refers to the outcomes, conclusions, findings, facts, information, discoveries, conclusions, or disclosures of learning. The "proces," on the other hand, refers to the methods, procedures, manners of thinking, techniques, strategies or skills involved in establishing the relevant facts or in coming to the relevant conclusions. Metaphorically speaking, we might say that the "product" of a form of knowledge refers to its literature, whereas the "process" refers to its language.[23] For example, a textbook of geology contains some part of the current state of geological knowledge (its literature), but this textbook need make no reference to the way in which geologists came to establish this knowledge (its language). The textbook represents the "product" of geological knowledge, while the investigatory procedures whereby geologists have established this knowledge represent the "process" of the discipline.

Let us turn now to the charge that the conventional curriculum is concerned with promulgating and assessing the "product" rather than the "process" of learning. As Kleinig puts it, using some of the concepts of Paulo Freire, "the teacher passes on a pre-packaged and relatively fixed body of knowledge to the student, and then determines how well that 'knowledge' has been assimilated."[24] No doubt historically the iniquitous policy of teacher "payment by results" led to a concentration on the assessment of mechanical, repetitive "product." The orientation of examinations towards "product" in the narrow sense of information recall is confirmed in more recent times by the study of the Leaving Certificate of 1967 by Madaus and Macnamara. This study revealed the importance of memorised knowledge not merely to pass but even to get honours in the examination.[25] But before adjudicating on the force of the criticism, something must be said on the place of product/factual knowledge in learning and assessment.

Every human skill or ability, from mowing the lawn, cooking, or practising surgery to the activities of the scientist and historian, can be said to contain a factual or propositional element, or an ingredient of "product" in terms of rules which can be formulated or put into words. As they are themselves theoretical activities, science and history offer "product" in the form of the facts or propositions which derive from the relevant enquiries in these disciplines. These facts and propositions (the "product") include formulae in science or mathematics or dates in history; in short, whatever facts are authoritatively established as a result of enquiries or "processes" conducted in terms of these disciplines. No sensible person would advocate that school pupils should be assessed solely or mainly on the basis of their ability to replicate facts or "product" which they have not understood. There are only very few educational tasks for which such learning is appropriate. Besides the alphabet, spelling, tables, and perhaps dates in history and geographical names, there is little in the school curriculum which can be communicated as simple propositions or "product."

But this does not mean that we can dispense with facts/product in favour of the pursuit of the procedures/processes of learning. Many human activities require a knowledge of facts, although they do not consist merely in the knowledge of facts. The study of science, literature or history requires that we master certain basic facts but the activity of solving scientific problems, doing literary criticism, or interpreting historical events involves using facts creatively rather than merely reciting them. In other words, it involves more than the learning of "product"— it also involves acquiring familiarity with the "processes" or skills of the subjects. Likewise, the vocabulary and syntax of a language can be represented as facts/product and in this form these can be incorporated into dictionaries and grammar books. Learning a language demands acquiring some mastery of its vocabulary and syntax, although it is not reducible to the learning of this "product." Even practical activities such as cooking or surgery involve knowledge of facts/product although, unlike in the case of theoretical activities, the goal of these activities is to realise certain practical goals rather than to manipulate propositions. The point of the foregoing is to show that much learning requires knowledge of facts ("product"), although it cannot be reduced to such knowledge. There is therefore nothing wrong with expecting knowledge of facts/product in assessing achievement in certain spheres; what is wrong is identifying significant achievement with mere knowledge of facts/product.

Let us then consider the criticism that the conventional curriculum, with its forms of assessment, promotes knowledge of "product" at the expense of "process." It seems at least implausible that conventional assessment is necessarily restricted to assessment of the lower order cognitive skills which require no more than the provision of information/product. Unfortunately we have only limited research on the Junior Certificate (or the Intermediate/Group Certificates) or the Leaving Certificate and, unfortunately, we are also told little enough officially about what the examiners require for successful achievement in these examinations. Nevertheless, until we have further conclusive evidence, we should treat with caution the view that these examinations are mainly a test of memorised "product" knowledge. No one familiar with the Honours Leaving Certificate, in particular, can be in any doubt as to the demands it makes on "process" knowledge. The examinations in the different subjects assess a wide range of higher order "process" skills. These skills require students to provide personal interpretation and analysis, to explain, to discuss, to defend arguments and to apply what they have learned to the solving of problems. Accordingly success in the Leaving Certificate cannot be plausibly dismissed as the mere skill in reproducing information which has been learned by heart without necessarily being understood. Students who do well in such subjects as English, history, physics or mathematics must show evidence of higher order cognitive "process" skills in order to engage in sophisticated reasoning of a discursive or of a mathematical character. Assessment of the conventional curriculum has therefore no necessary connection with mere information recall.

Yet the foregoing arguments must not be understood to detract from the value of the commendable efforts being made, particularly in the Junior Certificate, to place more emphasis on promoting the skills/processes of learning. The use of project work, field work, experimental work and historical research are all positive developments which will help young people to achieve greater mastery of the "processes" of learning. It is only appropriate that the forms of assessment take into account this aspect of learning. Nevertheless, the traditional curriculum has grave limitations and to these we now turn our attention.

Limitations of the Conventional Curriculum

There seems to me to be three major deficiencies associated with the conventional curriculum. These are its lack of precision with regard to objectives or desired learning outcomes, its tendency to neglect education in practical subjects and the arts and its tendency to neglect personal and social education.

What are Pupils Supposed to Know or To Be Able To Do?

The major deficiency of the conventional curriculum is its lack of precision with regard to what pupils are actually supposed to know or to be able to do as a result of engagement in particular subjects. The definition of subject aims and objectives or desired learning outcomes in Rules and Programme for Secondary schools is very inadequate. The relationship between the general aims of the curriculum and the aims of individual subjects has never been satisfactorily elaborated. The relationship between subject aims and syllabus content and the relationship between aims, content and examinations has not been closely articulated. Without a graded, ordered and discriminating definition of objectives or wished-for learning outcomes within subjects, as well as a systematic alignment of examinations with these objectives, the accreditative function of school learning remains imprecise. By contrast, what is learned during training for trades and professions has an obvious relationship to mastery of identifiable skills and areas of competence. But at secondary level it is not at all clear, for example, what grades in Junior and Leaving Certificate subjects actually mean when cashed out in terms of possession and skills and understanding.[26] Fine detail is not provided with regard to the level of understanding and skill which pupils are expected to acquire in a subject at primary level, at junior cycle and at senior cycle in secondary school and on how the different levels articulate or are linked with one another. Nor has the difference between what one is expected to know at pass and honours level been precisely specified. Introducing greater specificity with regard to objectives or desired outcomes, in terms of the achievement of understanding and mastery of skills, is partly a technical matter in curriculum design in which lessons learned from the use of modular and graded learning could be adapted to at least aspects of the conventional curriculum.[27] If we do not make it clear what we expect pupils to know or to be able to do, then we can hardly be surprised that some are less than fully committed participants in our school system. In fairness, we do find a commendable move in the identification of specific objectives or desired learning outcomes in the syllabi for the Junior Certificate and also in the very good syllabus for the Link Modules of the Leaving Certificate Vocational Programme.[28] But why have objectives or desired learning outcomes not generally been specified more tightly?

Admittedly there may be difficulties and indeed dangers in attempting to specify desired learning outcomes in large domains of knowledge or skill too narrowly or too exhaustively. But the main reason for the failure to be more specific about desired outcomes is due less to these difficulties and dangers and more to society's use of educational performance as a selection criterion for access to third level education and for high status employment generally. Once the instrumental function of education is fulfilled, then the detail of what pupils actually know or can do as a result of their education would not appear to be of enormous significance. And, of course, this situation leads to a tendency to neglect the education of those young people who do not aspire to third level education. More than a quarter of the age cohort does not sit the Leaving Certificate and only some 44% of the three quarters or so which take the Leaving Certificate manage to reach matriculation standard. But what is more significant is that 34% of candidates could not reach matriculation standard because they had not taken two honours subjects (23% all pass + 11% one honour only).[29] The lack of precision about what is actually taught or learned in school means that pass Leaving Certificate students are ill-served in terms of developing identifiable skills.

The Practical Domain

Another important limitation of the conventional curriculum is its tendency to neglect education in practical subjects and the arts. Among practical activities in Irish schools we have mechanical/technical drawing, woodwork/construction studies, metalwork/engineering, technology, home economics, arts and crafts, and music. Overemphasis on linguistic achievement can lead to a tyranny of the written word upon the educational experience of some young people. Where the dominant concern of the curriculum is with assessing competence in the use of the written word, what is learned at school tends to be bookish, passive and spectatorial rather than interactive and applicable to life.

One of the principal reasons for much of the neglect of the practical aspect of education is related to the exaggerated esteem attached to academic learning in general. The primacy given to academic learning is a feature of most educational systems; Ireland is certainly not unique in ascribing high status to such learning. Indeed historical evidence of this attitude can even be found in Egypt circa 2000 BC. In the famous text, The Satire on the Trades, an ancient Egyptian father exhorts his son to attend to his school work for fear he should end up having to work with his hands.[30] The neglect of learning in practical areas is also one of the undesirable features of education in Third World countries. The Third World, writes Theodore Lewis, "is filled with scholars who have abandoned rural agriculture, general education diploma in hand, only to become unemployment statistics in the cities." This is because education in the practical/technical spheres is "considered the education of last resort, a fate reserved for the academically unfit."[31]

This attitude is misguided from the point of view of promoting economic development and also from a philosophical and educational point of view. From a philosophical point of view, the identification of rationality with reasoning lies at the heart of negative attitudes towards practical subjects. But academic/theoretical subjects and practical subjects equally provide a context for the exercise of rationality. The activities of reasoning and doing can share predicates such as "clever," "accomplished," "careful," "painstaking" and "attentive." As the terms "reasoning" and "doing" go through the same "logical hoops," they can therefore be said to be analogous at least in these respects.[32] This is because only subjects of the same type can share predicates, therefore both between thought and action are expressions of human intelligence.[33]

It is important to acknowledge the educational value of practical subjects such as metalwork, woodwork, and other craftwork. These activities not only offer intellectual challenge but they can also make profound demands of our creativity. To some young people practical subjects may offer the most appropriate vehicle for creative expression, and to others these subjects may represent the only area in which they can engage in significant self-expression. Moreover, one emphatic finding of recent extensive research into the levels of satisfaction of young people with their schooling, on leaving school and then five years later, is of high levels of satisfaction with their education among young people who have done practical/manual/technical subjects in school.[34] In the context of these findings, the evidence of the wish of many traditional secondary schools to offer more manual/practical subjects is understandable.[35] It is regrettable therefore, as evidence shows, that the failure of these schools to provide manual/practical subjects is due to lack of the resources required in order to do so.[36] Indeed, by affirming the centrality of practical subjects, we are recovering one of essential educational traditions of Western civilisation. Practical activities, with roots in a tradition deriving from Christian, notably Benedictine, monasticism, have long had a place in Western education. The tendency to associate the conventional curriculum exclusively with learning of an academic/theoretical character derives from what is essentially a Greek tradition. By contrast, the monasteries of Christendom have always been places of labour as well as of learning, where manual and scholarly activities have been perceived as complementary features of life.

Personal and Social Education and the Development of Communicative Competence

A further negative consequence of the concern of the school with the written word is that it leads to a tendency to neglect directly addressing the personal and social education of young people in what I call its informative and formative aspects. The informative aspect would include, for example, the factual elements of sex education and information about career opportunities and the world of work in general. One essential dimension of the formative aspect of personal and social education is the development of communicative competence, that is, facility and confidence in communicating in the written and spoken word.[37] The relative failure of schools is this area is paradoxical given the traditional concern of school with language and literate culture. Three (English, Irish and French) of the four most popular subjects Leaving Certificate are actually languages. The linguistic orientation of the curriculum should contribute dramatically to the development of communicative competence. It is ironic that the dominant concern of the curriculum with competence at discursive writing does not lead to the development of communicative competence. Indeed, rating of their employees at the skills of written communication in a survey of 150 companies gives little grounds for confidence regarding the effectiveness of the school in actually teaching the skills of writing. None rated these skills as excellent, 10% rated them as very good, 40% as good, 42% as fair and 7% as poor.[38]

There are three main elements to the teaching of this communicative competence.[39] The first is a serious and sustained effort to improve the mechanics of written and oral communication. Included here would be the teaching of grammar, syntax and diction. The second is the teaching of creative writing and of literature. The third is the teaching of the dramatic and performing arts. Of course, it might be argued that the English syllabus traditionally contains these elements. But this syllabus has been dominated by the teaching of literary criticism. Awareness of the importance of oral communication and of wider forms of written communication is, however, one of the positive features of the new Junior Certificate. Nevertheless, more specific and systematic attention must be paid to teaching the mechanics of oral and written communication to all pupils. Remedial classes already benefit from this kind of approach to the teaching of literacy. In school it is vital to learn to compose various kinds of letters and curricula vitae and to perform other practical tasks in written communication. The second element to the teaching of communicative competence, creative writing, has also tended to be superseded by discursive writing, especially by literary criticism, which is given priority over the writing of stories and poems. Obviously it is important to learn to write discursive prose but this should not be at the expense of writing the poems and stories in which many young people delight. My impression is that the writing of stories and poems assumes a decreasing profile as pupils progress though the school system. The third element is the teaching of the dramatic and performing arts. At its most basic this involves learning the techniques of good self-presentation, not only at interviews but also in general social situations. It is important for young people to be taught how their speech and deportment convey to others an impression of their whole personalities. Improving the way they project themselves will prove of great assistance to young people in their vocational and personal lives. Drama and the performing arts have a crucial role here. This aspect of the curriculum is to be found in the teaching of English but it can be incorporated into the teaching of other subjects especially into the teaching of Irish and foreign languages.

My conviction regarding the importance of developing communicative competence does not derive from the study of philosophy and pedagogy. Rather it is born of my own experience years ago as an instructor/teacher on courses dealing with transition from school to adult and working life both in an AnCo/FÁS context and in the traditional school setting. One lesson which I have learned from several years experience of designing courses in transition from school to working life is the central relevance of the development of communicative competence. An anecdote which I was prompted to recall during a radio interview with Gay Byrne illustrates the point well.⁴⁰ Some years ago an employer remarked to me that a group of students (all academic low-achievers with negative self-images) on work experience had come to acquire a much greater self-assurance in the course of their placement with his company. This self-assurance, he observed, had led to major improvement in their performance at work. Later it was to strike me that the main reason for this change was due to the successful involvement of the students in producing and acting in James Plunkett's The Risen People which was part of their drama/communications programme. This experience reflects what has been found by curriculum designers in several of the countries of the European Community. Courses in drama and the arts can contribute hugely to the personal development of young people and thereby also increase their employability.⁴¹ By freeing young adults from some of their inhibiting self-consciousness, such courses have a unique potential to enhance self-confidence. I have found that there is no more potent means to enhance self-confidence than through the development of communicative competence.

The future is of its nature uncertain — to say this is a truism which it is tiresome to repeat and possible to exaggerate. What is certain is that communicative competence will always be an important feature of a fulfilled human life. The agenda which I propose for education is rather conservative: it is that schools realise in a more focused and sustained way their traditional aim to empower young through the written and spoken word.

This essay has moved a considerable distance from the introductory account of the nature of philosophy of education. In the course of the discussion, I would hope that the role and value of philosophy in educational discourse has not merely been asserted but also illustrated. The different arguments are now offered to the philosophical scrutiny of the reader.⁴²

POWER, PARTIALITY AND THE PURPOSES OF LEARNING

Pádraig Hogan

1. A New Metaphysics — Life as a Social Market

In the Middle Ages, theology was regarded as the supreme science. It gave to the contents of Christian Scriptures the status of incontestable truths. For instance, in his major work Summa Theologica,[1] Thomas Aquinas wrote: "it is impossible to use any truth to prove anything that contradicts our faith;" and also, "evidence adduced against the faith must be invalid evidence" (S.T. Ia, q1, a8). Theological accounts of reality governed not merely the conduct of the supreme science itself but also that of all other branches of learning. These had to bring their findings into conformity with what was decreed by papal authority as a single, theological world-view. The alternative was to invite papal censure and the unwelcome attentions of the Inquisition. The pursuit of learning enjoyed little in the way of sovereignty in those territories (most of them European ones) collectively known as Christendom.

Towards the close of the twentieth century, by contrast, the single world-view of Christendom is generally seen as just one stage, or more precisely as one era, in the development of Western civilisation; an era, moreover, which has long been eclipsed by other ones and by successive revolutions in politics and social organisation, in science and in industry. Far from a single world-view, modern Western culture is thronged with a multiplicity of contrasting world-views, and in most of the societies once associated with Christendom the power of the church as a social and political institution has waned to that of one interest group among others.

The contrast I have drawn here is a stark one. In doing so, however, I don't mean to suggest that there is now no recognisable body of beliefs and outlooks which can be said to have taken over the primary position of influence once enjoyed by the Christian churches and their teachings. In fact I would like to make the point that there is indeed such a predominant body of beliefs and outlooks, although it may not be as easily recognisable as the teachings and precepts of traditional religions. One might be initially tempted to say here that modern democracy, with its commitment to individual rights, due process and equitable procedures, supplies a basic moral-political creed for societies now characterised by a pluralism which grows ever more diverse. Insofar as it goes this would not be incorrect, but it presents us with a one-sided view only and masks something of greater significance. I am keen to highlight this other side, the less recognisable one, yet tacitly powerful one, and perhaps the best way to do this is by means of an analogy with religion.

The requirements of democracy could perhaps be described as the secular counterpart of the lists of "thou shalt" and "thou shalt not" commandments contained in traditional religious teachings. But theologians and most church authorities are now keen to point out that mere obedience to such commandments represents an impoverished or legalistic form of spiritual life. They claim that the person who loves God and neighbour with a sincere heart would embody the commandments as a natural expression of belief and commitment, as a way of life that was heartily embraced rather than reluctantly observed. And of course many might view democracy and its requirements in a similar manner. But history has shown that throughout the centuries countless religious believers experienced the requirements of religion not as a wholehearted commitment, but in a "god-fearing" way; namely as a decisive set of constraints on their more acquisitive impulses and desires. Of course the requirements of modern democracy and civic law provide nothing like the spiritual terrors through which constraints on thought and action were made effective throughout the long history of Christendom. Yet these modern requirements still serve a key function in providing their own constraints on acquisitive impulses. For instance, the leader who blithely disregards consultation and participation with others in decision making, jeopardises his or her own position as leader, particularly if that position is an office open to periodic election or review. Such a leader will invariably be accused of self-interest, of a selfish disregard of community interests and of the rights of others. The promptness with which accusations of this kind are nowadays made provides us with an insight into the tacit body of beliefs and outlooks which I am attempting to uncover. The first feature of this body of beliefs is the viewpoint, generally unadmitted where democracy must be seen to rule, that in dealings with others, each person is essentially in pursuit of greater advantage and power, either for self or for the grouping with which self is identified. Secondly, the prevalence of such a self-interested orientation gives interpersonal competition, whether declared or undeclared, a primary place in human action as such (and not merely, for instance, in fields such as sport and commerce). The corollary of this is that partnership, in any but a self-interested sense of the word, becomes a frequent casualty: still honoured in public utterance perhaps, but largely distrusted in practice. Where competitive motives are active, moreover, but cannot be openly declared, their suppression encourages clandestine attitudes and practices, such as vigilant suspicion, sectional espionage, or a preoccupation with equity which owes more to a spirit of ceaseless comparisons and jockeying for advantage than to any categorical commitment to evenhandedness. Thirdly, in an age where the advantages conferred by the possession of knowledge as a source of power often surpass those traditionally conferred by wealth, education receives a special significance as a desirable social good. But again, the tacit point is that this significance is now chiefly associated with education as a pathway to specialist knowledge, and thus to positions of increased power and influence. In other words, specialist knowledge here becomes important as a kind of inside knowledge; as distinct, that is, from a kind of knowledge which calls forth a person's unique promise, or fulfills a person's special potentials.

The outlines I have been sketching here suggest that behind the democratic avowals and observances of modern Western civilisations lies a moral-political ethic which, I believe, has become a predominant one: an ethic of competitive individualism, the more crass aspects of which are kept in some check by the institutions of democracy and the rule of civic law. These latter two features — democratic institutions and the due processes of law — have historically been acclaimed as virtues of Western "free" societies. The nineteen eighties, however, witnessed the remarkable proclamation in many of these societies of competitive individualism as a further virtue in its own right: the recasting of interpersonal life itself as a market. When the more unhappy consequences of such individualism are pointed out, particularly as they affect social and economic policy and the lives of communities and families which are less favourably circumstanced, it is often replied by its upholders that individual rights and liberties must be respected; that to do otherwise would be against the best interests of society as a whole; that it would be to abandon the legacy of the Enlightenment and to disregard the contributions to liberal political thought made by illustrious figures such as Adam Smith, Thomas Jefferson and John Stuart Mill. But in response to this kind of argument it must be pointed out that the constellation of beliefs and outlooks which constitutes competitive individualism in its *most modern* incarnation, owes its main character not to the Enlightenment, or to any thinker associated with political liberalism or classical economics. Rather the essentials of this body of outlooks are to be more properly found in the writings of an isolated German figure whose works were largely peripheral while Marxism enjoyed a central place on the international political stage, but whose observations and pronouncements can now be seen in many ways to be uncannily prophetic. The thinker in question is Friedrich Nietzsche. This might seem a shocking or even an outrageous suggestion to those who would like to adopt competitive individualism as a child of democracy and liberal thought. All the more reason then that Nietzsche's theses on power now merit a particular claim on our attentions if we are properly to understand the quality of public discourse, the tenor of decision-making and, not least, the purposes of education, in the world's most modern civilisations.

2. Seven Theses on Power

My outline of competitive individualism has been necessarily brief. What I would like to do now therefore is to put before you seven recurring theses from Nietzsche's writings and then consider how closely or otherwise these theses describe the motives and patterns of conduct which are the predominant ones in modern pluralist democracies, including our own country. I should add here that Nietzsche's works contain many more theses than the seven I have chosen, and that my selection, though it seeks to be representative, cannot claim to be comprehensive.

The first thesis calls into question, and indeed seeks to discard, the traditional notions of objective truth and objective knowledge. It asserts that objectively true accounts of the world and of humankind are impossible; that all accounts are *interpretations* and that such interpretations are invariably coloured by the background and the particular interests of the person or party giving the account.

The second thesis follows from this and can be called Nietzsche's perspectivism. This maintains that knowledge is possible only as a perspective knowing; or in other words, that every philosophy, theory or viewpoint advanced about the world and humankind's place in it, is only one among many possible alternative perspectives or interpretations. Nietzsche is keen however to distinguish perspectivism from relativism. Relativism would hold that nothing can decide what perspectives are better or worse than any others. So perspectivism, unlike relativism, has to produce some kind of criteria to distinguish better perspectives from inferior ones. Nietzsche gives no systematic account of such criteria but insists instead that they would arise in the course of a wholehearted acknowledgement on the part of each individual of what was most "life-advancing," most "life-preserving" and most "species-preserving," namely, what he boldly calls the "will-to-power." With this we have come to the third thesis.

The third thesis can best be put in Nietzsche's own words: "A living thing desires, above all else, to vent its strength — life as such is will to power." In recurring passages of his works he asserts that falsification, exploitation, envy, and lust for domination, pertain inescapably to life as such and not merely to primitive societies. In one such passage he writes:

> Life itself is essentially appropriation, injury, overpowering of the strange and weaker, suppression, severity, imposition of one's own forms, incorporation and, at the least and mildest, exploitation.[2]

Nietzsche is annoyed however that words such as these, which, he insists, describe a necessary part of life's unfolding and progress, and which often serve to identify the strong and courageous from the weak and mediocre, should have about them such a bad odour. Eighteen centuries of morality and religion are seen by him as the cause of this state of affairs, so the fourth of Nietzsche's theses to concern us is his critique of Christianity.

Nietzsche's passionate dislike of Christianity is expressed in declarations such as the following: "One may without exaggeration call it the true calamity in the history of European health"[3] To those who were strong and powerful, according to Nietzsche, Christianity preached that they should be ashamed of their domination of the weak. To the weak it preached "thou shalt obey" and that their weaknesses should be seen as virtues (e.g. meekness and lack of courage should be recast as humility; herd mentality as love of neighbour). To the sick and wretched, according to Nietzsche, Christianity preached that they alone were to blame for their miseries, which were to be seen as punishment and atonement for sinfulness.[4] The ascetic ideals of Christianity Nietzsche viewed as a conceited masking and perversion of a more basic motivation, namely the will to power. On such ideals he wrote:

> Here rules a *ressentiment* without equal, that of an insatiable instinct and power-will that wants to become master not over something in life but over life itself, over its most profound, powerful and basic conditions.[5]

In summary, the fourth thesis asserts that Christianity is nothing other than ecclesiastical politics as a form of the will to power.

The fifth of Nietzsche's thesis which I have selected for consideration attacks Christianity, not for the contents of its teachings but for the dogmatic character of these teachings. In other words, in Nietzsche's view, these teachings have been offered not as one interpretation of the world and humankind; nor are those to whom they have been preached been left free to accept or reject them. Rather, Nietzsche insists, they have been proclaimed as the final truth about the whole of reality, and such proclamation has furnished itself with powerful means to enforce its own will and to suppress any awareness that what it proclaims is just an interpretation.[6]

The sixth thesis concerns the search for knowledge, including self-knowledge, which Socrates had placed at the centre of all serious enquiry. In Nietzsche's view, however, Socrates is to be faulted because his conception of self-knowledge was not radical enough. It still acquiesced, according to Nietzsche, in acknowledging a requirement for a universal morality (i.e. one that was binding on all) and, despite its criticisms of conventional moral practice, it still retained a deferential attitude to traditional morality. For Nietzsche then, Socrates failed to acknowledge the primacy of the will to power. Accordingly, the kernel of the sixth thesis is to be found in the following declaration from Beyond Good and Evil:

> I do not believe "a drive to knowledge" to be the father of philosophy, but that another motive has, here as elsewhere, only employed knowledge (and false knowledge) as a tool. For every drive is tyrannical : and it is as *such* that it tries to philosophise.[7]

In brief, whereas for Socrates, the chief significance of knowledge lay in emancipating people from ignorance, for Nietzsche, knowledge was power, or more precisely, the capability to extend and vent one's power.

The seventh and final thesis describes the kinds of moral criteria and actions (though "moral" would hardly be Nietzsche's choice of word) that spring from what Nietzsche urges as an unflinching and courageous embrace of a world shorn of the illusory comforts provided by philosophy, religion and morality. Paraphrasing Nietzsche's arguments, the kind of standpoint indicated here would, in the first place, be a wholehearted acceptance of all the horribleness, and the marvellousness, of drives and desires which now thrust themselves forward and back in human experience in all their naked, elemental character. It would, secondly, be a sustained attempt *to create one's own values;* to make one's own prowess confer a meaning on one's actions; indeed to fashion one's own life as a bold, autonomous and original work of art. And thirdly, this would mean giving originality of direction and strictness of discipline to those particular drives which, in any particular individual, enabled him to stand out and pursue distinctiveness and greatness, to become in a word, a superior kind of human being, or *Übermensch*.[8] (Nietzsche dismisses females from these kinds of possibilities). Moral considerations, insofar as they are present here, are largely taken over by aesthetic ones, and receive their character from them. This is precisely the inversion of values which Nietzsche seeks to promote. He readily admits that the distinctiveness and greatness that beckon the human spirit here might indeed alternate with downfall and torment. He insists, finally, that all "free spirits" who embrace greatness in this way know and accept that they must live dangerously, that their greatness, moreover, is inevitably doomed to mortality and extinction.[9]

3. Partiality, Partnership and the Purposes of Learning

For reasons that time won't allow us to go into here, it is all too easy to write Nietzsche off as a crank, an eccentric, even a madman. The reassurances offered by such a dismissal are however all too facile. Within the present century alone, abundant historical and sociological evidence can be called on to give substantial weight to most of the seven theses we have considered. If we reach back beyond the present century, moreover, Nietzsche's theses seem even stronger, particularly those dealing with religion. In fact the burden of such evidence can sometimes be so pressing that conclusions such as Nietzsche's seem inescapable. I am keen to argue, however, that just where some of Nietzsche's insights come closest to being most illuminating, they also come closest to obscuring the heart of the matter. Despite his criticisms of dogmatism and despite his discerning remarks on knowledge as interpretation and perspective, the vehement insistence and all-inclusive character of many of Nietzsche's key arguments leave little room for interpretations contrary to his own. Such a contrary interpretation might argue, for instance, as follows: that purposeful human action might be occasioned *not just by one* primary source, but by two, or possibly more primary sources. And against Nietzsche's more sweeping declarations one can put forward a more subtle thesis, however, than this example just cited.

This more subtle thesis — which can find even greater support in historical and biographical evidence than do Nietzsche's theses on power — would deny absolute primacy to any single drive or desire; it would hold that most human beings rarely act from one primary motive, but more usually *from a mixture of motives,* or indeed from a conflict of motives which may be only partially resolved. Such motives could of course include power and self-interest, but could also include, to mention but a few, service to others, acknowledgement of one's identity and of one's particular contribution to human engagements, a desire for tolerant co-existence, compassion for suffering and bereavement, loyalty to friends or family, solidarity with the downtrodden, or indeed love of God and one's neighbour. The central point in the case I am attempting to put forward here is that human experience is characterised by an ever-unfolding play of motives, rather than by any primary motive which must be accorded a permanently fixed position at the top of a hierarchy.

Now this conception of human experience as a play, or more precisely an *interplay* of motives — in our engagements with others or with the ideas and thoughts that are addressed to us — has a crucial importance for how we understand the purposes and the practice of education. It provides us firstly with an understanding which is both practical and dynamic, as distinct, for instance, from more theoretical conceptions such as "man as a rational animal," man as "homo economicus," or man as a "res cogitans."[10] Such theoretical conceptions, no less so than Nietzsche's declarations on the will to power, tend to give a fixed priority to one aspect of the interplay I have just mentioned, or even to obscure the point that our experience is indeed just such an interplay. Secondly, our conception of the purposes of education is further advanced if we understand human experience not just as an interplay of motives but also as an interplay of perspectives, beliefs, interests etc., each of which may have something distinctive to contribute, but also, each of which is in itself partial. Thirdly, we are now in a better position to see that even the most accomplished of human expertise and judgement, the most inspired aspiration, commitment, and so on, still represents only a partial, a provisional and indeed a fallible understanding. Far from promoting any relativism, this awareness provides the enterprise of education with a unique and a distinctive orientation; an orientation which views teaching and learning in any field as a disciplined venturing forth of the best efforts of imagination, intellect and sensibility; a venturing forth whose best fruits warrant no vanity or opinionatedness, but serve rather to provide human understanding with a refined modesty, with an educated sense of its own capabilities and limitations. This is an orientation, moreover, which is defensible in a universal sense and which is entitled to claim an accountable sovereignty in relation to the concerns of state, or church, or commerce, or indeed social expectations more generally.

I am keen to recall here a remark made by Socrates during his trial, as it captures in a concise way the kind of orientation which I am attempting to describe:

> Real wisdom is the property of God, and this oracle is his way of telling us that human wisdom has little or no value. It seems to me that he is not referring literally to Socrates, but has merely taken my name as an example, as if he would say to us "The wisest of you is he, who has realised, like Socrates, that in respect of wisdom, he is really worthless."[11]

If all who have a sincere and abiding commitment to education were to acknowledge that in respect of wisdom we are not so much "really worthless" as radically incomplete, or inescapably limited by the partiality of perspective, then the orientation towards enquiry which I am attempting to describe would, at the same time be an orientation towards greater completeness, while recognising that completeness in any absolute sense is not possible for humans. In a word, it would be an orientation towards dialogue. And this would apply just as much to policy-makers and managerial parties as it would to teachers, parents and pupils. But what would such an orientation look like in practice? I will try to summarise some of its chief characteristics in the following list:

1. A readiness to listen in a disciplined way to what the other party has to say, including that party's strongest criticisms of one's own standpoint;

2. a readiness to grant that there may be distinctive insights and points of merit in the perspectives of the other party;

3. an ability to discern and a willingness to note the most significant points in the other party's perspectives, including any points of agreement with ones' own standpoint, any points of difference, and any areas of new ground;

4. a capacity to bring one's own standpoint incisively into play and to explore in a self-critical way the merits of the various perspectives which have been offered by the different parties;

5. a willingness to put the claim to truth in one's own perspective at risk, in the effort to achieve a more inclusive understanding.

These five essentials describe an orientation towards dialogue which is quite different from what is often referred to in everyday talk as "discussion and dialogue" — i.e. bargaining and negotiation. I should add, moreover, that the orientation I am describing has clearly an aspirational character and that, as such, its overcoming of the preoccupations of bargaining will be more a matter of degree than any final achievement. As an aspiration, moreover, it involves not so much a naively idealistic programme but rather a sincere effort to join the continual play of influence in human affairs: to try to make significant inroads on the currents of partisanship, to provide an impetus in a contrary direction from that of individualism. If such efforts are not made in a renewed and a committed way by education, it is hard to see where they will be made in any significant way at all.

In conclusion, I would like to leave you with six summary theses of my own, which proceed from the orientation I have been exploring and which are of practical relevance to the concerns of policy-making in education at all levels. I would argue that these are particularly important for any educational discourse in a democracy which wishes to be defensible, and seen to be defensible; that is, which wishes to put itself beyond the charges contained in the seven theses on power considered earlier.

First Thesis : Wherever educational authorities presume proprietorial rights on the sensibilities of the young, even from the most altruistic of motives, the educational enterprise is disfigured from the start: the emergent identity of the pupil is cast in an inflexible mould and much of what is most promising and special among each pupil's potentials is obscured or smothered. A mentality which places a primary emphasis on proprietorial rights, moreover, albeit for the most sincere reasons, promotes an ethos of power-seeking, overlooks the to-and-fro interplay of teaching and learning, and undermines the very concept of education as a partnership.

Second Theses : Properly viewed, teachers' efforts with their students represent overtures on behalf of one or other of the voices of tradition within the different fields of human accomplishment. These overtures can be properly made only by teachers in whom the subject in question speaks with fluency and engaging conviction. Such overtures can rarely or ever be neutral, but they can in defensible measure be honourable and open-minded, just as they can in a defensible way embody strict requirements and demanding expectations. All of this calls for insightful and courageous educational leadership in schools and colleges, and for accountability in appointing candidates with the best credentials to leadership positions.

Third Thesis : The experience of curricula should be sufficiently broad in the primary school and junior cycle of secondary school so as to address the full range of aptitudes and potentials of each pupil. Equity requires, moreover, that such experiences should be equally available to all, and that resources should be judiciously allocated with this criterion in mind. Positive discrimination to offset disadvantage may regularly be a feature of such judiciousness. Specialisation should proceed only when a particular family or cluster of potentials has been identified as a person's most promising ones. Parents and teachers have to co-operate actively and continually on this. Specialisation should never be such, however, that a student becomes systematically schooled in one or other exclusive range of perspectives, to the continual neglect of contrasting or contrary ones. Bearing in mind these points, benefit to the pupil, rather than any territorial claims of different subjects for preferential treatment, should be the overriding criterion here.

Fourth Thesis : The legitimate purposes of assessment are concerned not with providing a test of ingenuity in beating an examination system but rather with evaluation of the quality of the curricular experiences offered in school: with assessing the fruits of those experiences not just under one main heading such as the strategic recall of and deployment of information, but under headings which would include the following benefits of learning: the pupils' ability to solve problems, to be incisive and consistent in tracing inferences and conclusions, to deal in a fluent way — in writing and speech — with concepts, theories, linguistic idioms and images, to discriminate between key issues and minor ones, to identify the focus of a genuine question and to keep that focus continually in view, to carry out a piece of practical work which incorporates an intelligent conception and a high standard of execution, to show the fruits of purposeful co-operation with fellow students, to advance a coherent and consistent case supported by well-chosen evidence, to show that they understand the significance of what they have studied for their own emergent potentialities and inclinations, for their own sustenance and sense of identity.

Fifth Thesis : Where the management of schooling is concerned, it matters less what the formal composition of the managing authority is than that this authority should contain a variety of perspectives, (e.g. founders, teachers, parents) as distinct from a preponderance of one perspective; it matters less, moreover, what the precise makeup of the authority is than that this authority should recognise that the responsibilities of partnership summon energies towards dialogue and the mutual education of perspectives rather than towards factional rivalries; it matters less, finally, what the representative composition of the authority is than that all its members be sufficiently courageous and sufficiently well versed in the basics of a defensible educational philosophy, so as to safeguard a responsible exercise of the sovereignty of learning on the part of the school or college and its teachers. A Teaching Council would also have a key part to play in such safeguarding, as it would in the articulation of a professional code of ethics based on a defensible educational philosophy.

Sixth Thesis : If educational efforts, governed by the five essentials of dialogue described earlier, concentrated on identifying and cultivating each student's ownmost potentials, and on nurturing a durable sense of identity and community in harmony with those potentials, there would be a closer match between the natural talents of a population and the kinds of economic activity which were most fruitful for that population. This would call for a greater scope and authority to shape and to make crucial decisions locally. But it would also give priority to the educational talents and aptitudes of persons over the so-called needs of the economy. This order of priority would, moreover, be much more promising, even in terms of economics and the nurturing of resilience and enterprise, than is the utilitarian metaphysics which is now being internationally urged on schools, often with an urbane plausibility, but yet with an insistence scarcely less relentless than that of the world-view of an authoritarian church in the Middle Ages.

QUESTIONS AND DISCUSSION — SESSION TWO

CHAIR: Dr. Peter McKenna

PANEL: Dr. Joseph Dunne
Dr. Kevin Williams
Dr. Pádraig Hogan

Peter McKenna:
Can I ask any intending contributors to identify themselves before speaking and to speak closely into the microphone, as the discussion is being recorded.

Eoin Cassidy (Mater Dei Institute):
I'd like to address this question to Joe Dunne. He presented a very intelligent paper, enlightening us as to the range of burdens placed on schools by society, and also the complex relationship between schools and the economy. I want to raise for discussion an issue which was at the heart of his paper, namely, the relationship between intrinsic and extrinsic forms of education. I want to examine this by looking at two related but distinct ways in which the goals of education have been classically expressed; that is the relationship between the goals of excellence and efficiency. Excellence in this sense incorporates a vision of the Good. Efficiency incorporates a vision of the workable, the successful, and perhaps ultimately, what leads onto the growth of power. Certainly the relationship between excellence and efficiency is one which permeates philosophical

discourse from the earliest of times. It finds its classic expression in Plato's Dialogue *Gorgias*. The question is whether something is efficient because it is excellent or whether it is excellent because it is efficient. I want to suggest that the challenge you posed to us this morning Joe, to recover a sensitivity to the intrinsic goals of education, is one which unfortunately may perish on the rock of this most deep-seated desire in human beings to be efficient, to be successful, and ultimately to be the centre of power.

Joseph Dunne:
I don't think that we should try to define excellence by efficiency, because that really begs the question. In other words, in order even to be efficient, you've got to have something that you're efficient towards; you've got to have a purpose already defined. Now I wanted to define the purposes of education as something that couldn't adequately be addressed in terms of efficiency. The relationship between extrinsic and intrinsic rewards, of course, cannot entirely be broken, and I didn't try to break it. We do have to earn our crust. There are things which necessarily concern us as beings who have to survive. But keeping the focus on practices, and on what I called the goods internal to practices, that doesn't lead to inefficiency. In many ways, the kinds of inefficiencies we have in our society arise because practices aren't in good order; in other words because the real purposes of the enterprise aren't kept clearly to the centre. And of course you're right about human nature. We are all prone to these acquisitive desires and power cravings, and perhaps (with other more positive inclinations, also, of course) they will always be there. And any philosophy which doesn't recognise them is superficial and shallow, and doesn't really have much to contribute. So there is the question of disciplining those, and one of the attractions of that notion of a practice, with the central notion of intrinsic goods, is that the more that people can be brought to those, (and that's what education is about for me) the more they engage in just that disciplining of these acquisitive things that Pádraig also was talking about. But it's always a battle, the battle in education is to do just this and I certainly wasn't trying to suggest that it was easy.

Pádraig Hogan:
I am concerned that with schooling at the moment, efficiency tends to be all, and that outlooks associated with the points system for entry to higher education aggravate this view. These outlooks are very different from the classical view of excellence, which included a vision of a Good. Modern views of excellence, by contrast, tend to the view that you're a somebody if you perform well, regardless of what at; you're a nobody if you perform poorly. And this is a variant of the disturbing modern metaphysics — the metaphysics of power — that I've been talking about. I am concerned at the extent to which this is catching hold in our own society. I'm not saying, however, that it has caught hold completely. There are marvellous cultural influences working in our society, including in our schools. But the schools are subjected to such contradictory pressures that they may present more a picture of confusion than coherence. And here I'm reminded of the lines Brian Friel attributed to the schoolmaster in *Translations:* "Confusion is not an ignoble state." In such a confusion we have to keep the push going for what is decent and defensible from an educational viewpoint, as against the tidal pressures for an efficiency which is informed — explicitly or implicitly — by considerations of self-seeking and power. By international standards, I would still think that our schools are better than many in this regard.

Peter McKenna:
Some very interesting issues have been put to our reflections here. Are there any more questions or observations? Yes, Kevin?

Kevin Williams:
I'd like to make a comment on the distinction between doing things for extrinsic or instrumental reasons, and doing things for their own sake. There's quite a literature on this. Perhaps two points should be made about the distinction. If we're talking about the motivation of individuals for involving themselves in certain activities or practices, I'm a bit concerned about the way that base motives are attributed cavalierly to the young people of the country: "they're only doing it for the points." How do we know that? I don't think that we are privy to what other people's motivations are, in the way that some commentators think we are. And my second point is this. I can't see

why we can't accept that we act from multiple motives. Our motives are inextricably mixed. For instance, fifteen years ago I might have been aspiring to get on the Dublin football team just to win an All-Ireland medal. But I might also have been aspiring to get on the team because I wanted the excitement of playing football. People's motivations are mixed and why can't we leave it at that?

Peter McKenna:
There is another contributor on this issue?

Dr. Gerry Gaden (UCD):
I want to take up this issue of extrinsic and intrinsic motivation. I don't think that the real point that was being made earlier was about the motivation of pupils. It wasn't so much a question of why the pupil did this or that. It was more a question of why certain sorts of educational decisions should be made. The question has really to do with: Do we decide what ought to be done in schools on the basis of considerations which are external to education, or are there a set of criteria internal to education by which we can make these decisions? In other words, we might decide to put certain things on the school curriculum, or to teach certain things in certain ways because that benefited the economy, or because it promoted some other aspect of our society's life. And that would be an extrinsic reason. Now I thought that what Joe Dunne was drawing attention to was the question of whether there are considerations internal to education which could lead us to make our educational decisions in one way rather than another. And that is quite independent of the question why particular pupils should do one thing rather than another. Perhaps you could comment on that.

Joseph Dunne:
I think that's right. I think also that a practice itself declines if extrinsic considerations predominate. There is then a real loss. And I think we ought to have the means of recognising the loss. If you start playing fast and loose with what the real demands of a practice are, because your eye is on something else, then the whole centre is lost. That's the main point.

Gerry Gaden:

Could I just come back on that for a moment. Yes that's so, but I do think that we probably need to do a lot more work to try and get clearer about what the internal goods are. Joe pointed — very eloquently — to the need to do that kind of work, but I think the work was not itself done in what anybody has said this morning. You could put the question in various ways. You could ask for instance, "Could somebody emerge from school into adulthood with a whole lot of conditions satisfied — for instance a person who is sane, healthy, economically productive, employable and so on — in short, with all these external goods; is it possible for a person to emerge in that sort of state and yet for us to say that this person is not educated?" If we can say that, then we need to ask what is being left out, what is being missed. And these will be the goods internal to education. But I think we need to do an awful lot more to identify what these might be.

Peter McKenna:

I think you are asking a really profound question, and it comes back in a sense to what can be evaluated by assessment. How does one track the various intra-personal and interpersonal aspects of development? Portfolios are one way of doing it, but again these can become very mechanistic. Any comments from the panel on this?

Kevin Williams:

Can I just say that I don't consider that the question of intrinsic and extrinsic is just a question of human motivation. What I did say is that it is sometimes represented as being simply a question of motivation. It's a much more complex issue than this, and one on which more work has to be done. But let's dispense with this question of motivation first.

Peter McKenna:

There is a further question from the back of the theatre.

Ita Mc Grath (primary teacher):

I agree by and large with Pádraig Hogan's conclusions, but I would like to focus on his third one. It deals with the pupil's experience of the curriculum but it seems to have a cut-off point at the end of the post-primary junior cycle, and I wonder why there, because I would like that style of education he describes to continue to the end of second level, and thus reduce the influence of the points system further. Because the points system, to my mind, seems to be based on an acceptance that the student wants access to university, or the banks or other highly sought-after career, and it ignores entirely the fact that such careers want young able people. So do universities want able students. If we perceived it that way maybe then we could further develop the idea of a broader education which focuses on the potentials of the individual student rather than merely on the individual's ability to score points on a narrow test.

Pádraig Hogan:
It's a vast question. I would share your concern about the points system and the stanglehold it puts on educational experience, particularly in the senior cycle of post primary schools. I expect that over the next few years an enormous amount of work will have to be done to make inroads on this. The NCCA has commenced it but the work is still only in its infancy. Those teachers who are earnestly working with the Junior Certificate at the moment are attempting to continue a focus — on the educational experience and the uniqueness of the pupil — which lies at the heart of the primary curriculum. But there is a change of heart and a change of pedagogy required in this, more especially so as this focus extends into senior cycle and confronts the traditions which have long been established there. When we look at the potentials and fluencies which were nurtured by innovations such as the Humanities Curriculum, we can see here a tradition of some two decades at the junior cycle of post-primary, which is in keeping with the focus I'm talking about. Unfortunately, it was a marginal tradition for many years and only with the advent of the Junior Certificate have the better practices of this tradition slowly begun to find their way into post-primary schools more widely. This kind of practice has to be developed into senior cycle, and assessment procedures have accordingly to be designed to catch a broader range of abilities and fluencies and benefits. Putting it in terms of "the goods internal to education," assessment procedures have to be tailored, and curriculum experiences have to be provided, which will give each emerging young adult the best opportunity to give as adequate an account as possible of their potentialities, fluencies,

aptitudes; as the person they actually are. Now that is an enormously complex and difficult job. These goods that are internal are not a fixed catalogue for all. They may vary from one person to another. If we concentrate as a society on the goods that are internal to education, moreover, the economy won't have to feel neglected, because the goods in question would include resilience, initiative, self-confidence, and other potentials which were left undiscovered or smothered by the points system cum assessment system as it is at present. There's many a person working as a banker or doctor who might have been far better in a different occupation, had their best potentials been discovered, and assessed, and certificated in a different way in the senior cycle and in university. The difficult work that lies ahead stretches also into third level and I would hope that we can look forward to authoritative help from statutory bodies — such as a Teaching Council for teachers, and similar bodies for other occupations— in providing curricula and assessment procedures for students which are in keeping with the aptitudes that are most naturally their own and with their emergent occupational talents.

John Doyle (primary teacher):
I would like very sincerely to thank the various speakers. It's wonderful to hear the different idioms and the different ways in which questions are explored. I want to speak about one point in primary schools. In many cases there are still entrance exams for secondary schools. I see these as a kind of colonisation of the primary school by the secondary school. This is not a colonisation of the educational system by the economy. Rather, it is education turned against itself. And I notice that in the last two years of the primary school there is a very serious distortion, because the entrance exams begin early in sixth class, and this means that the pupils have to a double year (fifth and sixth) while in fifth class. This means a profound distortion of both fifth and sixth class. There are of course primary schools that don't experience this and they find it hard even to imagine it. But the point I want to emphasise is that this situation seriously distorts the pupils' experience of education. In fact I'm not sure what the word education even means in this context. And secondly, it also distorts the teachers' experience as educators. They have to suffer the deep anxieties of children and their parents. The idiom appropriate to discussing education wilts and withers here.

There is no need to discuss the intrinsic goods of education when the task laid upon the primary school is so obvious: "Get those children through. Get them into the schools that their parents demand." That is how the primary school is going to be judged. And I'm saying that here is an image for the children of what lies ahead for them later on with the points system. In the primary school they are already learning that education is assessed not on its own merits, but extrinsically; by performance in a very narrow range of exams. The only teachers who are really outside of this dark shadow are the teachers of the infant classes. In the Junior Certificate, these pupils may again experience something of a brief paradise, but they have already been branded. They have already learned too early that education is for the narrow bottleneck. Now I am wondering if the panel can address any remarks which I can carry back as it were; a word of illumination on the tensions I have been describing.

Joseph Dunne:
If there is a hopeful sign that you can bring back, I think you have already adverted to part of it yourself towards the end of your remarks. In one sense the stranglehold is reaching downwards — into the primary school and down through the classes. But if we take the Junior Certificate as the focus of change within the secondary system we can also see a push in the opposite direction to that which you have identified. There is a real push now in an upward direction, for reform of the senior cycle. That is where a lot of the important action is at the moment. I would have thought that the work being done by the NCCA — particularly the changes which are being explored for the senior cycle — signifies a lot of important rethinking. It's not as open I suppose to public discussion as it might be, though in a way it is, but not very many participate in it. How successful it will be in changing the senior cycle remains to be seen. The other thing I might say by way of assuaging concern over entrance exams is the change in the population structure. In some areas now there isn't the same scramble as there was to get into secondary schools. And in some cases post-primary schools are now in a situation where they have to go out and look for people. And that will act to take some pressure away from primary schools.

Kevin Williams:

I'd like to say something in response to John Doyle's comments. I think that there is a danger in exaggerating the extent to which young people are engaged in the so-called search for points. Before they come to Leaving Certificate, more than one quarter of the age cohort has left school. So these aren't competing for points. And secondly, although almost three quarters of the age cohort do the Leaving Certificate, a third of these candidates does not aspire to matriculate. This is because they have taken no honours subject (23% of candidates), or just one honours subject (11%). So it's not as if the whole age cohort is trying to matriculate. If you put the two points I've mentioned together you find that one half of the age cohort in sixth class in primary schools will not aspire to matriculate. These figures indicate that the "scramble for points" is not of universal concern to our school-going population. Whether everyone should aspire to matriculate is a question for another day.

Peter McKenna:

We have three questions pending and I think that will take us up to time.

Louis O' Flaherty (post-primary teacher):

My questions link a few things together. I came here to be informed. And I think all of us in education have to listen and learn from each other. Last night I heard Barney O' Reilly put the question "Do differences in religion always warrant different educational provision?" And that was dealt with somewhat in Eoin Cassidy's presentation, though I found difficulty in following all of it. At the end of it he seemed to be in favour of everything. He put an addendum in and said that for those who had a secularist view of education, he would be in favour of them having provision, provided they went out and smoked in the back yard, or something; provided they didn't mix with the others. Maybe I'm doing him an injustice, but he's here and maybe he'll go through me like a knife through butter if I'm wrong. I listened today and I heard various people say that we are in an evolving situation. Bearing this evolution in mind, I think there actually is a consensus view of what constitutes a broadly liberal education. Whether such a consensus is described as "ideological," or "rhetoric," or "philosophy" is beside the point. I come with this view that all experience is learning. I liked what Pádraig was saying about the five essential points of dialogue, and I think dialogue is essential to education. But if we are going to say "You cannot come into this institution unless you buy the total package, and if you don't want the total package we will give you a little place aside, so long as you don't disturb us," then I think this a denial of dialogue. And there cannot be an educational way forward with this kind of position. The viewpoint I'm putting is not atheistic or anything like it. In this day and age we must, as a society, be prepared to have the kind of multidenominational provision which enables schools to debate with openness the cumulative knowledge and contrasting world-views which have come down to us;. to argue the toss without a triumphalism which declares that now that socialism is gone we have all the answers and are back to phase one. Does anyone want to comment on that?

Peter McKenna:
Would it be better to take the remaining two contributions from the floor and then call on the panel to answer. Yes? O.K. Sorry, the remaining three contributions.

Ann Mc Nulty:
Mr. O'Reilly outlined last night the parallel development of schooling and economics. And it is clear that because these have been organically linked, the idea of work (that is, getting a job) seems to be the goal of education. Anything less seems to be regarded as failure. Dr. Dunne asked this morning what are the effects on education now that it is the decisive agent in determining pupils' economic future. My comment is that the demoralising effects of unemployment may have their roots in our present educational philosophy, which seems to be based on an out-dated work ethic. Is there any place in current educational philosophy to prepare pupils for the possibility of unemployment, which is the reality of ordinary life for many. If the ordinary is central to the culture of modernity, as Mr. O'Reilly argued, should the schools not also prepare pupils for the possibility of a life of leisure, which might be viewed in a positive way. After all, in previous societies, the leisured classes were the elite.

Pacelli O'Rourke (teacher):
Several times over the course of last night and today, the distinction was drawn between education and schooling. In that regard, I was intrigued by Gerry Gaden's question: "When the person comes out with all the attributes and so forth, how do we know that he or she is educated?" The chairperson didn't articulate a response, nor did he wish to or intend to, but he did mention assessment and portfolios. And it just brings to my mind the thought that I honestly think that most of us involved in education have an inflated idea of the significance of schooling, as part of the education process of a human being. I still honestly think that we see schooling almost as the whole process. We are talking at length about intrinsic and extrinsic motivation, whether it is of the pupil or of the system itself. In my own younger days as a teacher of religion, I used to assume far too much responsibility for the way these young people were going to turn out in their relationships with God, with each other, in the quality of their adult lives and so on. These were very dangerously inflated aspirations and I found that I was getting ever more frustrated, until someone told me that what I needed was the ability to care and not to care. And I just offer that as a piece of small "p" philosophy today.

Dr. Joseph McCann CM, (St. Patrick's College, Drumcondra):
I'm trying to practice the five essentials of dialogue that Pádraig put forward. If we take it that education is the development of a personality or of the individual, or of the human being, and schooling as that which a society, or a community, or group, is prepared to devote to education, and if we hope that what happens in schools is sometimes educational; it seems to me then that it becomes important to know, from a philosophical point of view, from an ideological point of view, and a theological point of view, what a human being is capable of. This brings us directly to the notion of potential and this underlying concept is what I found to be most interesting about this morning's three papers. The most disturbing point is the vision of Nietzsche, of what an individual developing a potential can in fact mean. But what I didn't hear discussed today, what lies behind the Green Paper, and what worries me, is the fact that over the last thousand years there have been at least four changes in the view of education. That is, the move from —

(a) seeing people as making a living and playing a role in a traditional community, to

(b) taking a job in a factory in the early industrial revolution, to

(c) following a career in life, which I think is the post-War concept of career guidance: that students would make their own choices and pursue an occupation which they found personally fulfilling, to

(d) the last stage, which is the one that is upon us and which envisages that each person should take responsibility for his or her own living, and making his or her own living if possible even by creating a new enterprise or a new job.

And the educational system could help people to do just that. I think this is an area of consensus that people will have to come to; will have to give their energies to how that is achieved.

Peter Mc Kenna:

Can I just ask the members of the panel to respond to the contributions just made, and then Dr. Hogan, as President of the ESAI, will close the symposium.

Joseph Dunne:

Well, in response to the points raised by Joe McCann, which also relate to the question put by the lady who spoke just before him, I think it would be very provocative to say that you were going to prepare people for unemployment, and I don't think any one had in mind that schools should set out to select those who will be unemployed. But there is a real issue here which we might not be quite clear on. How much longer can we go on with the older system of employment, or expectations of employment; for instance the steady job which you take up when you leave school and which you hold till retirement at sixty-five. I think Joe McCann's last point was referring to a change in this pattern. I think that the traditional model is now very questionable, and our inability to provide it is becoming ever clearer. Whether the numbers of unemployed at present is just a temporary thing or a deep structural change is a major concern. The industrial society may have been capable of providing full employment. The post-industrial society may not — at least not in the traditional sense. But even if this is the case, I don't think it means that we have to have a permanent under class. The way in which we can go into and out of work over a lifetime can become much more flexible.

There are straws in the wind here, if we look at career-breaks, flexitime, work-sharing and the like. But of course the whole question of how income is to be distributed will need to be radically re-examined. And within this context, I think that education could be expanded in a way that is very desirable. Adult education, for instance, which we haven't mentioned here at all, deserves a huge amount of attention that it doesn't get. And I think it is here that the humanities have a special role to play, because it seems to me that older people may be in a better position to profit from say literature, history and so on. I'm not saying that people in their teens and early twenties can't, but there are huge opportunities for these kinds of benefits later on. And because of the way that people had to plug into full-time work it made it very difficult for them to find opportunities for further education. But in any case, even if people do remain unemployed, I think it is a responsibility of their education to give them something that is still worthwhile to themselves; that they can actually be profitably involved in some kind of enterprise.

Turning now to the other question, the one about schooling and the denominational issue, I think there are very good arguments for the kind of non-denominational — or multi-denominational — system which is inclusive. In answer to the first question you posed on that — it was also posed by Barney O'Reilly last night: "Is a division of schools along denominational lines always justified?" I don't think one could argue that separate schooling is always justified. The state sets many conditions for recognition and funding in the case of all schools. And I can imagine a situation where a church or other group should not be allowed to have its own schools. But the justification for not allowing it would have to be very carefully spelled out — in terms of its violating some overriding or compelling requirement of institutions in a democratic polity. Short of such an extreme case, I think what you are trying to balance on this issue is catering for what is common and having a pluralism *within* schools on the one hand, and on the other catering for difference and having a pluralism *of* schools. I think there are necessary trade-offs there. I think that what you get within the denominational school, what you get that is valuable— or what some people believe is valuable and I would tend to agree with them — is a stronger notion of the good that is religion. I'm not necessarily saying that it is a better notion of the good, but it can be lived out in a fuller way because there is an expressed commitment there. So I think there are benefits in that. I can see that there are also benefits in the other pattern, in terms of bringing children together from different backgrounds, and in that sort of mixed environment, letting them learn from each other.

Kevin Williams:

There was a very large number of issues raised, and some of them stray into the area of social commentary where I wouldn't feel particularly competent. As I am not able to see into the future, I am not sure that I would have anything to say about the future of work. Yet I would point out that within the Irish post-primary system since the late seventies, there have been efforts, particularly at senior cycle, to prepare young people for a future where there won't be traditional paid employment. That's just a matter of record, if you look up the various curriculum initiatives such as the Transition Year Option and the Vocational Preparation and Training Programme. An account of these can be found in *Achievement and Aspiration:* curricular initiatives in Irish post-primary education in the 1980s which was published by the Drumcondra Teachers Centre. Although I'm not a person who likes to engage in general social commentary, particularly platitudinous statements about the future, I always have a suspicion that things don't change as much as people sometimes assume. Around 1870 — at a time when one would have thought that there was plenty of conventional paid employment — John Ruskin said "You complain of the difficulty of finding work for your men. Depend upon it the real difficulty rather is to find men for your work. Look around at this island of yours and see what you have to do to it." That was over a hundred years ago. I think that this is still the case today and I suspect that it will remain so for the future.

With regard to Louis O'Flaherty's point on denominational schools, I'd broadly agree with what Joe Dunne has said. But one concern I have is that if we had exclusively secular schools young people might never be exposed in a genuine way to the good that is religion. One thing which I've observed from experience is that it is not very difficult to expel religion from people's lives. I come across many young people in this country who are totally indifferent to religion. If we had exclusively non-denominational or secular schools as distinct from multi-denominational schools, this situation might become worse. A school principal in this city recently said to me— "One of the reasons we like to encourage young people to go to religion class, and in fact to attend school liturgies, is that some do not encounter religious practice outside of the school." The only exposure these will get to religion as a good in human life is therefore in school. I'd be concerned that if young people were not exposed to religion in school, they might never encounter religion as part of human living. There is also an argument that young people have a right to an education in religion. By this I mean an initiation into religion as part of human living — not simply the academic study of religious beliefs. Of course, in this country parents have a constitutional right to withdraw their children from religious education in the formative sense. There is an obvious tension between the rights of children to receive as comprehensive an education as possible with regard to the goods in human life and the rights of parents to exclude them from religious education. This is a large issue but I suspect that the rights of children in this respect have not been sufficiently to the fore in discussion of the matter. Perhaps we might return to the subject in a future ESAI symposium.

Pádraig Hogan:
I'll confine myself to the question of religion and schooling. With regard to the point about different kinds of provision, as a society we simply have to try to move towards some kind of consensus on this. Kevin and I might disagree somewhat on the merits of consensus, but maybe not ultimately. Our resources for schooling are far from limitless and the praiseworthy achievements of our different kinds of schools have much more in common than they have in opposition. At this late stage of the twentieth century then, we will have to come together again, and again, and if necessary again, to "argue the toss"

honestly and openly, as Louis O'Flaherty said, and see what measure of agreement is possible — if resources are to be judiciously deployed and if we are not to squander the extra educational opportunities for pupils which such deployment would make possible. The National Education Convention and the recent Round Table discussions in Dublin Castle were a very encouraging start in this regard, but events seem to have taken a few discouraging turns since then. We have to make better efforts than we are making at present to learn something of the discipline of dialogue. We can of course, as different "partners" in education, go in and demand that we retain the separate rights that our party traditionally enjoyed and we can insist that legislation will give us nothing less than these demands.

That kind of activity, despite the justifications it can provide for itself (legal and otherwise), will be perceived by most of the population at large as a jockeying for advantage in a game of power politics. Is this what the benefits of education are really about? Is this what the good of religion is about? Yet this seems to be what it is most visibly about. It is not surprising that large numbers of young and not-so-young people, when confronted by such examples of the good intrinsic to religion or education would say "no thanks" and follow extrinsic rewards which beckon in a very tangible way. By contrast, I think that "the good that is religion" finds itself in more hospitable circumstances, certainly from an educational point of view, if it is communicated from *below* as it were, with no presumptions being made about the pupils' loyalties. The analogy here is with the teaching example of Jesus Christ. He had no legal guarantees. He chose quite different teaching styles depending on whether his listeners were "disciples" or "multitudes." In all cases the only power he had was the compelling authority of sincerity and the imaginative ability to see practical illustrations for his teachings everywhere in everyday life. When speaking to "multitudes" (i.e. a pluralist gathering) moreover, his success lay chiefly in the fact that he made no prior assumptions about their convictions in matters religious. Where religion is concerned, we would do well to remember that "multitudes" are probably more common than disciples in our schools today, including our denominational schools.

Conclusion
It remains for me to thank you warmly for attending and contributing to the symposium. Thanks to the chairpersons Professor Áine Hyland and Dr. Peter McKenna; to the four students from Mater Dei who voluntarily took care of registration; to you the participants — many who are teachers, many who are representatives of the religious orders, the teachers' unions; the parents, including in a major way the National Parents Council. There were some absences, which were commented on earlier. And indeed some notes of regret were received from people who expressed a desire to be here but who had prior commitments, including the Minister for Education. In any case, thanks to all of you who did come along. I'd like to say a special word of thanks to Dr. Peter McKenna. It was simply a joy to work with someone who was so co-operative and who had the thoughtfulness to anticipate all the various things which needed to be done. He arranged in a very warm-hearted way to put some of the best facilities of this modern university at our disposal.

Finally, the proceedings of the symposium will be published. All of the five presenters had to curtail their papers, to allow the discussion sessions to be scheduled. But the full versions will appear in the book of proceedings, as will all the contributions to the discussions. We would hope to publish the book before the end of the year or early in 1995. Our response to the Minister's call for a philosophical debate will thus become a matter of public record, but also, I hope, a rich and lively record which will be regularly consulted.

Notes

Introduction

1 See the publications *Issues and Structures in Education* (1984) pp12-14, Dublin : Curriculum and Examinations Board. Reconstituted as the National Council for Curriculum and Assessment, 1991.

2 See, for example, the NCCA documents *The Curriculum at Junior Cycle* (1991) and *Senior Cycle: Issues and Structures* (1990). The former document acknowledges criticisms that philosophical issues have been left implicit in curriculum provision in Ireland, p.3, but declares that weaknesses of this kind have already begun to be addressed in the reforms to the curricula of the junior cycle of post-primary education. See also *Education for a Changing World* — Green Paper Ireland 1992, Dublin : Stationery Office.

3 The text of the Minister's lecture "Towards a Coherent Philosophy of Education," is published in *Irish Education — Decision Maker,* Issue No. 8, Spring, 1994.

4 J. Coolahan (Ed.) *Report on the National Education Convention,* Dublin : Secretariat of the National Education Convention, 1994.

NOTES

Barney O'Reilly's Paper

1. The *Report on The National Education Convention* states, p.15, "The proposals for educational change in early nineties do not represent a period adjustment or trimming of the system, they involve fundamental change in the way the Irish educational system works." The Minister for Education in 1992 John Marcus O'Sullivan lecture stated"... we cannot afford an outcome where we are all once more in five or ten years time initiating this debate yet again in yet another futile attempt to bring some focus and order to the path ahead." *Irish Education Decision Maker,* No.8, p.5. These are assessments with which I agree.
2. Dr. John Sheehan of UCD is the most regular in his treatment of the economics of education. For a recent paper by Dr. Sheehan see *Irish Banking Review,* Autumn 1992, "The Economic Relevance of Irish Education : An Emerging Debate." Dr. M. O'Donoghue of TCD works extensively for international agencies, e.g. OECD 1990, *Review of National Policy for Education — Norway.* In 1941 W.K. Riordan presented an M.A. thesis at UCD entitled "Education as Investment" — *Investment in Education,* 1965, the Report of the Survey Team appointed by the Minister for Education in October, 1962, was the first major overview of the economics of Irish education. Martin O'Donoghue's Ph.D thesis at TCD in 1967 *Education : an economic problem of resource allocation* built on his work as a member of the survey team. *Analysis of Public Educational Expenditure in Ireland* was presented for a Ph.D at UCD in 1970 by J. McCabe who worked under the supervision of Patrick Lynch, leader of the Survey Team. Other publications

include: McDonagh (1977) "The Way the Money Goes" in *Oideas, No.17*, and Tussing (1978) *Irish Educational Expenditures — Past, Present and Future* and Barlow (1981) *The Financing of Third Level Education* were both published by the ESRI. NESC Report 95, *Education and Training Policies for Economic and Social Development* (1993) is the most recent major enquiry in this area which includes (i) the financing of education and (ii) the contribution of education to economic development. It is to be noted, however, that neither economics nor politics of education appear among the categories identified by Sugrue and Uí Thuama in their recent paper on postgraduate educational research in Ireland: Sugrue, C. & Uí Thuama C. (1994) "Perspectives on Substance and Method in Postgraduate Educational Research in Ireland," in *Irish Educational Studies,* Vol.14, pp102-129.

3. The Political Studies Association of Ireland was founded in 1982 with the object of promoting the study of politics in Ireland and of the study of Irish politics in general. The Association forwards the interest of the discipline by organising an annual conference and publishing a yearbook *Irish Political Studies.* For an account of the development of "political studies" as an academic study in Ireland see Committee of the Political Studies Association of Ireland (1992) *Political Science in Ireland,* Limerick: PSAI and Coakley, J. (1991) "Political Science in Ireland : development and diffusion in a European periphery" in *European Journal of Political Research,* No.20, pp359-373. An overview of the current state of the academic study of politics in Ireland can be gleaned from Coakley, J. & Gallagher, M. eds. (1993), *Politics in the Republic of Ireland,* Dublin: PSAI Press and Hill, R. & Marsh, M. (ed), 1993, *Modern Irish Democracy,* Dublin : Irish Academic Press.

4. O'Buachalla (1989) *Education Policy in Twentieth Century Ireland,* Dublin : Wolfhound Press, had its origins in a Ph.D study in Politics Department TCD and provides the starting point for future studies. The public hearings and ample reporting of the National Education Convention have made the politics of education a little more public. I am in some sympathy, however, with the view of O'Sullivan, D. that "while the debate proceeds with unsensed constraints, the grandiose

self-deception that we are participating in open analysis, with everything on the table, remains unthreatened" in *Studies*, 83, 330, Summer 1994, pp191-199. "Hands up all in Favour of Inequality."

5. A summary survey (for this paper) of post graduate courses in education at universities in the Republic showed only one institution formally includes the economics of education in course outlines. None explicitly addresses the politics of education. The appearance of "Educational Policy Studies" suggest a movement towards the study of the politics of education in some institutions.

6. However papers by P. Hogan mean that these issues have not been totally neglected by philosophers of education. See for example, Hogan, P. (1990) "What makes Practice Educational" in *Journal of Philosophy of Education*, Vol.24, No.1, pp15-26, and Hogan P. (1992) "The Sovereignty of Learning, the Fortunes of Schooling and the New Educational Virtuousness" in *British Journal of Education Studies*, Vol.40, No.2, pp134-148. The work of sociologists such as Denis O'Sullivan and Kathleen Lynch has also focused on the philosophical dimensions of educational dilemmas. See especially O'Sullivan, D. (1989) "The Ideational Base of Irish Educational Policy" in Mulcahy, D.G. & O'Sullivan (eds) *Irish Educational Policy : Process and Substance*, Dublin : Institute of Public Administration, O'Sullivan D. (1992) "Shaping Educational Debate : A Case Study and an Interpretation" in *The Economic and Social Review*, Vol.23, No.4, pp423-438; Lynch, K. (1988) "Counter-Resistances in Education : An Examination of the Relationship between State Managers, Social Classes and Educational Mediators" a paper presented at the International Sociology of Education Conference, Birmingham, 1988, and particularly, Lynch, K. (1989) *The Hidden Curriculum : Reproduction in Education, an appraisal*, Lewes : Falmer Press.

7. In the course of discussion following delivery of this paper at DCU (23/9/94) a participant enquired as to the import, for the theses adopted in this paper, of the growth of informal adult education outside the schooling system, which must, however, be considered to be part of the "education system." I would suggest three pertinent observations. Firstly, the existence of

such a sub-set of the education system does not invalidate the positions taken in respect of schooling, because of its relative size. Far and away the greatest portion of education is conducted under the aegis of the schooling systems. Secondly, much of the informal adult education takes place within a framework of public provision, utilising classroom type groupings and public examinations for evaluation and validation. Thirdly, attitudes and values which are most likely to be evident in the processes of adult education are also more likely to be present among those who have had the benefits for a schooling system in the first place. See Inglehard, R. (1990) *Culture Shift in Advanced Industrial Societies,* Princeton, N.I.: Princeton University Press, p.66, f.f. or a discussion of "the rise of post-materialist values," and Whelan, C.T. ed (1994) *Values and Social Change in Ireland,* Dublin : Gill and MacMillan, p.166 f.f. for the relationship between post-materialist values and educational qualification in contemporary Ireland.
8. Quoted in Hamilton, D. (1990) *Learning About Education : An Unfinished Curriculum,* Milton Keynes : Open University Press, p.37. For an interesting paper on the phenomenon of "domestic education" in Ireland, see Logan, J. (1988) "Governesses, Tutors and Parents : Domestic Education in Ireland 1700-1880." Domestic Education 1750-1800 "A Preliminary Investigation" in IES, Vol.7, No.2, pp1-19.
9. The ideas in this section are drawn heavily on Hamilton, D. (1989) *Towards a Theory of Schooling,* Lewes : Falmer Press, particularly Ch.2, "On the Origins of the Education Terms Class and Curriculum," Ch.4, "Adam Smith and the Moral Economy of the Classroom System," and Ch.7, "Notes Towards a Theory of Schooling."
10. See Taylor, C. (1989) *Sources of the Self : The Making of Modern Identity,* Cambridge : Cambridge University Press, p.285, f.f. Taylor's major work posits three interlinked characteristics of "modern human identity'" — (i) a heightened sense of 'inwardness' of the self, as the source of sensibility and moral judgement, (ii) a view of nature 'as an inner moral source,' ("from this perspective, a central part of the good life must consist in being open to the impulse of nature being attuned to it, and not cut off from it," p.372) and (iii) the

affirmation of ordinary life. The new valuation of ordinary life in general and commercial life in particular, can be traced, according to Taylor (pp285-6) "in the recession of the aristocratic honour ethic," being replaced by a 'bourgeois' outlook which stressed "the goods of production, an ordered life, and peace — in short the activities of ordinary life." Economics which "focuses on the interchange between humans and nature as a domain with its own laws ... cannot be seen just as a 'scientific' discovery that people stumbled on. It reflects the higher value put on this dimension of human existence, the affirmation of ordinary life," p.286. The new science (of economics), in its notion that the "events in this domain form a self-regulating system ... of production and exchange is a prime manifestation of the interlocking providential order of nature," p.286. This idea of economics as a part of nature and nature as a 'moral source' helps explain the engagement and moral commitment that is not infrequently associated with economic discourse.

11. To recognise as unsustainable claims of economists and political scientists to be able to uncover by (value free) scientific methodology the 'laws' which govern the operation of economic and political systems does not vitiate the validity of economics or politics as the object of study. What is at issue here is the nature of the knowledge claim made by these areas of study. See Bellamy, R. (1993) "The demise and rise of political theory" in Bellamy, R. (ed) *Theories and Concepts of Politics,* Manchester : Manchester University Press, pp1-16. The suggestion that "an adequate political theory must seek to integrate the philosophical analysis of the concepts we use to think about politics with the empirical investigation of political processes and social structures" ibid. p.13, underpins the suggestions in this paper. The presence of "oppressive and self-deceiving tendencies" (from Dunne, J. 1991 "The Catholic School and Civil Society") in capitalist societies may be facilitated by the 'hegemony of scientific-technical reason' rather than caused by it. It is my contention that the elevation of the mundane and the ordinary, implicit in the rise of capitalism and democracy, is in fact more significant than their temporary containment as disciplines within the paradigms of scientific — technical reason.

12. For detailed analyses of the processes in the emergence of modern educational systems see Archer, M. (1979) *Social Origins of Educational System,* London : Sage; Hopper, E. (ed) (1971) *Readings in the Theory of Educational Systems,* London : Hutchinson De Swaan, A. (1988), *In Care of the State,* London : Polity Press and Muller, D.K., Ringer, F. & Simon, B. (eds) (1987) *The Rise of the Modern Educational System,* Cambridge : Cambridge University Press.
13. The question of the extent to which the relationships between systems of politics, economics and schooling are characterised by a *determining* role for economics as a *base* or basic system for which politics and schooling as super-structures, or whether they are systems characterised by 'relative autonomy' are issues which I do not propose to pursue in this paper, other than to state my own position which is to attribute to each a measure of autonomy which means that while it is significantly influenced by the others, no one can be said to determine the other. Neither the correspondence theory of Bowles and Gintis which link Schooling and Economy in deterministic modes nor the view of Chubb and Moe who propose strict independence between schooling and the political system, seem to me to be adequate. See Bowles & Gintis (1976) *Schooling in Capitalist America,* New York : Basic Books and Chubb & Moe (1990) *Politics, Markets and America's Schools,* Washington D.C. : The Brookings Institution.
14. Elbaz, F. (1983) *The Practical Knowledge of the Teacher,* Lewes : Falmer Press, was an important stimulus to my reflections. For a review of current scholarship on this issue see Emberson, J.W. (1993), "Teachers Thinking and Reflective Teaching : Issues for Teacher Training in Ireland" in *Irish Educational Studies,* Vol.12, pp122-123.
15. For the most comprehensive exploration of these concepts and others pertinent to an understanding of the professional knowledge of teachers see Dunne, J. (1993) *Back to the Rough Ground : Phronesis and Techne in Modern Philosophy and in Aristotle,* Notre Dame University Press.
16. See Lonergan, B. (1958) *Insight : A Study of Human Understanding,* London : Longman, pp173-244, pp279-316.

17. It is in the propensity of decision-makers to be influenced by interest, bias, sloth or chance or lack of time, and thus fail to seek the answer to that unanswered 'pertinent question,' that I locate the source of oppression and self-deceit. As much a problem for philosophers as for administrators, politicians or economists.
18. See Brennan (1991) "Christian Education, Contestation and the Catholic School" in McCormac, T. (ed) *The Catholic School in Contemporary Society,* Dublin : CMRS, p.11 and MacIntyre, A. (1981) *After Virtue,* London : Duckworth, p.29
19. The following set of assumptions are outlined in a text currently used in undergraduate economics courses: "Pareto-Efficiency. Four assumptions are central to the following analysis:
    (i) the aim of policy-makers is the maximisation of social welfare;
    (ii) social welfare depends positively upon the welfare of individuals in society;
    (iii) the welfare of individuals depends upon goods and services that they consume;
    (iv) individuals are the best judges of their own welfare and act in their own self-interest.
    Pareto-efficiency can be decomposed into *efficiency in production* and *efficiency in exchange.*" from John, A. (1991) "Primary Policy Objectives" in O'Hagan, J.W. *The Economy of Ireland : Policy and Performance* (Sixth Edition), Dublin : IMI, p.56. These assumptions seem to me to be eminently in need of some philosophical reflection before an edifice of policy is built on them.
20. See Dunne (1991) op.cit. pp27-28 where he uses 'ideology in this way: "... the official ideology of reason" — 'an ideology which is still entrenched in most of our curricula and institutional arrangements.'
21. For consideration of the different senses of the term ideology see Thompson, J.B. *Studies in the Theory of Ideology,* Cambridge : Polity Press, pp1-16, also Williams, R. *Keywords,* London : Fontana, pp153-157, and Therborn, G. (1980) *The Ideology of Power and the Power of Ideology,* London : Verso.

22. See Hogan, (1983) "The Central Place of Prejudice in the supervision of student Teachers," *Journal of Education for Teaching*, Vol.9, No.1, pp30-45, in which the author argues that to *understand* is to *interpret* "by bringing our prejudgments to bear ..." He goes on to identify two classes of preconception/prejudgements: those inspired by popular fancies, ideological influences or world views and those "which deliberately seek to be tentative and open to rational modification in the light of new encounters ..." p.40.
23. It has not been possible to carry out a systematic and comprehensive survey of recent Irish work in the philosophy of education to support the categorisation presented here. It is proposed to test it against the judgement of the conference audience.
24. Papers such as Swan, D. (1990) "Play, Practicality and Policy in Irish Education," *Irish Educational Studies*, Vol.9 and Williams, K. (1992) "Usefulness and Liberal Learning" in Lane, D. *Religion Education and the Constitution*, Dublin : Columba Press, pp34-59, appear to me to come into this category. In his presentation to conference, K. Williams instanced papers by Gaden and by Williams himself which argued for the place of technological and practical subjects on the curriculum.
25. In my view Murphy, D. (1988) *Martin Buber's Philosophy of Education*, Dublin : Irish Academic Press, comes into this group.
26. Recent examples include Brennan, N. (1989) *Education and Relevance for Life*, in New Syllabi, New Learning, Dublin : CMRS; D. Murray (1991) *A Special Concern the Philosophy of Education : A Christian Perspective*, Dublin : Veritas, and Bradley, B. (1994) "Philosophy and Religion in Irish Education," *Studies*, 83, 330 Summer 1994, p.143. Cassidy, E. (1992) "Irish Educational Policy in a Philosophical Perspective : the Legacy of Liberalism" in Lane ed. *Religion, Education and the Constitution*, Dublin : Columba Press, pp60-83. Papers by Brennan, Dunne, McDonagh and McCormack, T. ed. (1991) *The Catholic School in Contemporary Society*, Dublin : CMRS, may also be included in this general group.

27. A related point is made by Sugrue, C. & Uí Thuama, C. (1994) "Perspectives on Substance and Method in Postgraduate Educational Research in Ireland," *Irish Educational Studies*, Vol.13, pp102-128. "Narrowness of substantive foci and methods of enquiry have serious implications for the nature and conduct of research, the health of the teaching profession through inservice provision; for the quality of teaching and curriculum change; for teacher educators and researchers as well as policy makers. It is vitally important that these issues be thoroughly discussed as part of the process of educational reform and particularly in the context of creating new subnational structures in the system, which will create additional demands for new forms of educational leadership and expertise," pp124-125. Speaking of the history of education in recent decades, Logan, J. (forthcoming) suggests that "... its vast bulk and growing bibliography contrasts with the limited range of issues which they explore," *The History of Education in Nineteenth Century Ireland*, p.9.
28. See Hogan, P. (1992) op.cit. p.144.
29. See Memorandum V.40, issued by the Department of Education, 1942.
30. See Barber, N. (1989) *Comprehensive Education in Ireland*, Dublin : ESRI, Paper No.25.
31. I cite the history of the Group Certificate examination in support of this position.
32. Article 6 and Article 40 of the Irish Constitution contains the articulation of these positions as currently apply in the Republic of Ireland, Article 6 states: "All powers of government legislative, executive and judicial, derive, under God, from the people, whose right it is to designate the rulers of the State, and, in final appeal, to decide all questions of national policy, according to the requirements of the common good." There appears to be an ambivalance at the heart of our constitution when this article is considered alongside the preamble which opens: "In the name of the Most Holy Trinity, from Whom is all authority and to Whom, as our final end, all actions both of men and States must be referred ..." Article 40.1 states: "All citizens shall, as human persons, be held equal before the law. This shall not be held to mean that the State shall not in its

enactments have due regard to differences of capacity; physical and moral and of social function." The references to "differences of moral ... and of social function" are made more concrete in Article 41.2.1 which states: "In particular, the state recognises that by her life within the home, woman gives to the State a support without which the common good cannot be achieved." For a discussion of the implication of these articles for equality and protection from discrimination in employment see Fennell and Lynch (1993) *Labour Law in Ireland,* Dublin : Gill & Macmillan, pp156 ff. The special position given to the Catholic Church under the terms of Article 44.1.2 was another example of a distinction formally acknowledged — until its removal in 1972. For a general discussion of equality see Baker, J. (1987) *Arguing for Equality,* London : Verso. For a discussion of the implications of these ideas for education see Lauder, H. (1991) "Education, Democracy and the Economy," *British Journal of the Sociology of Education,* Vol.12, No.4, pp417-431, also Johnston, G.L. (1991) "Liberty Equality, Fraternity : democratic ideals and educational effects," ibid, pp483-499. It is a little disconcerting to hear a Minister for Education state that she wanted "... to be remembered as the Minister who recognised that different groups of people have a different ethos and different rights." — Quoted in Irish Times, 13/9/1994.

33. The contested nature of our understanding of these processes is well illustrated in the recent publication : Brady, C. ed (1994) *Interpreting Irish History,* Dublin : Irish Academic Press.

NOTES

Dr. Eoin G. Cassidy's Paper

1. See Eoin G. Cassidy, "Irish Educational Policy in a Philosophical Perspective — The Legacy of Liberalism," in *Religion, Education and the Constitution,* edited by Dermot Lane, Dublin : Columba Press, 1992, pp60-83, esp. pp60-64.
2. In *Decision Maker,* No. 8. Spring1994. pp4-10.
3. In *Studies,* Vol. 83, Summer 1994, pp143-152.
4. The validity of Bradley's criticism and the importance of this issue is implicitly acknowledged in section 3:1 of the background paper for the N.E.C., in *Report on The National Education Convention* edited by John Coolahan, Dublin : National Education Convention Secretariat, 1994, pp149-150. See also ibid. P.7.
5. Bruce Bradley, "Ghostly Rhythms" in *Studies*, Vol. 83, Summer 1994, p.148.
6. *Education for a Changing World,* Dublin : The Stationary Office 1992, pp33-34.
7. *Primary School Curriculum: Teachers Handbook Part 1,* Dublin : The Stationary Office 1971, p.23.
8. *Education for a Changing World,* p.90.
9. In the *Primary School Curriculum: Teachers Handbook Part 1,* the religious dimension of human life is seen as critical in determining the focus of education. Note the following quotation from Chapter 1 entitled "Aims and Function," "Each human being is created in God's image. He has a life to lead and a soul to be saved. Education is, therefore, concerned not only with life but with the purpose of life, And, since all men are equal in the

eyes of God, each is entitled to an equal chance of obtaining optimum personal fulfilment,"p.12. The contrast with the Green Paper could not be more marked. In section 4:2 which treats of the aims of the Primary School curriculum, the only reference to religion is the following passage placed sixth in a list of seven aims, "(to) Develop an understanding of their own religious beliefs and a tolerance for the beliefs of others,"p.87. Even if one was to compare this statement in the Green Paper with that contained in the much more recent *Report of the Review Body on the Primary Curriculum* (PCRB), Dublin 1990, one could not fail to notice the same shift in emphasis. Under the heading of "Specific Aims,"p.11, the PCRB document includes the following statement, "To help children to acquire and develop moral and religious values and a respect for the beliefs and values held by others." In contrast to this statement there is no evidence in the Green Paper of any recognition of the educational value of assisting children to acquire and develop moral and religious values. There is a significant difference between assisting students to understand their own religious beliefs and assisting them to acquire moral and religious values. Only the latter gives recognition to the importance of these values — one's to which the Green Paper is allegedly committed to fostering. See *Education for a Changing World,* p.33. Furthermore, in its treatment of the objectives of the Primary School curriculum in the chapter entitled "Aims and Objectives of the Primary School Curriculum", the PCRB document both acknowledges the importance of the spiritual development of the student and recognises the integrated nature of human development (including the spiritual) in ways that are markedly absent from the Green Paper. See The *PCRB Report,* pp11-12.

10. The most serious instance of the downgrading of the place of religion at Junior Cycle level can be seen in the way in which the Green Paper treats of the issue of the "Core" subjects in the curriculum for the Junior Cycle (p.94). Surprisingly, religion does not appear on this list. In drawing up its list the authors of the Green Paper accept, with one exception (the inclusion of Technology), the list recommended in the recent (1991) NCCA position paper, *The Curriculum at Junior Cycle,* Dublin, 1991. However, intentionally or otherwise, they fail to alert the reader

to the fact that in the NCCA document which they are following the only list of core subjects discussed is one for the Junior Certificate (See p.12). This misrepresentation of the NCCA document has serious implications for the place of religion on the Junior Cycle curriculum. One would hardly expect religion to feature on the NCCA list of core subjects for the Junior Certificate, but to suggest, as the Green Paper does, that in keeping with the recommendations from the NCCA it should not be a core subject on the curriculum at Junior Cycle level is an entirely different matter. Not only does it misrepresent the NCCA document but it totally ignores the recommendations of the Curriculum and Examination Board as set out in *Issues and Structures in Education*, Dublin, 1984, pp15-20. On the broader issue of a core curriculum, See Malcolm Skilbeck, "The Core Curriculum," *The Curriculum Redefined: Schooling for the 21st Century*, OECD Documents, Paris: OECD 1994, pp95-100.

11. See *The Curriculum at Senior Cycle: Structure, Format and Programmes,* National Council for Curriculum and Assessment, Dublin, 1991, where in section 5:2 under the heading "Principles of Senior Cycle Education" it includes the following reference to "the centrality of the intellectual, moral, physical, social and spiritual development of each individual student,"p.9. In addition, section 9:9 states that "Provision should be made at senior cycle for Religious Education, for Physical Education and for Guidance and Counselling." The document elaborates this reference to religious education in the following passage, "Religious Education: it is envisaged that religious education would be offered to all students. The development of a course in Religious Studies for Leaving Certificate as an option should be considered further,"p.22. The recognition accorded to the importance of religion at Senior Cycle level by the NCCA is reinforced in their submission to the NEC entitled *Curriculum and Assessment Policy: Towards the New Century,* Dublin, 1993, p.54 and 60.

12. The importance attached by the Minister for Education, Ms. Niamh Bhreathnach, to the process of dialogue and the issue of transparency can be adjudged from the content of her opening address to the NEC, which includes the following, "My invitation to you to participate in this Convention is a tangible recognition

of the importance of openness and transparency in the policy-making process and/or the involvement in this process of all of us who contribute to education." *Report on the NEC*, p.218. This emphasis on the importance of transparency is repeated in her concluding address to the Convention, ibid., p. 242. See also the opening and concluding speeches by the Convention Secretary-General Professor John Coolahan, ibid. esp. P.236.

13. See *Education for a Changing World*, "Introduction," pp3-5, and the section entitled "Challenges for the Future," pp37-40.
14. See the concluding address by the Minister for Education, Ms Niamh Bhreathnach, to the NEC in *Report of the NEC*, p.243, the submission by the Department of Education to the NEC in *Presentation to the National Education Convention*, Dublin, 1993, p.5, and the detailed treatment of this issue in the *Report of the NEC*, pp31-33.
15. See the report by the Education Committee of the Irish National Teachers Organisation *The Place of Religious Education in the National School System*, Dublin, 1991, pp4-6 and 34-36. See also the *INTO Response to the Green Paper*, Dublin, 1993, pp79-81. In particular note the following recommendation from this latter document, "The INTO favours the inclusion of Religious Education on the primary school curriculum. ... Religious Education would imply, in effect, education about religion as distinct from nurture in a religion," p.79.
16. For a detailed treatment of the issue of Indoctrination See Jeff Astley, *The Philosophy of Christian Religious Education*, Alabama : Religious Education Press 1994, pp44-77.
17. Note the following passage from the response of the Teachers Union of Ireland to the Green Paper. The response is titled *Equality in Education*, Dublin, 1993 : "In the turbulent world of today the tragic consequences of cultural and religious intolerance are depressingly easy to see, not least on this island. While the TUI acknowledges that such conflicts arise from a multiplicity of factors, we are fully committed to multi-denominational schools as a necessary antidote to intolerance," p.6.
18. This vision is expressed in the joint response of the Catholic Bishops and the Conference of Major Religious Superiors, titled *Education for a Changing World, The Green Paper on Education — Ireland — A joint submission from the Irish*

Bishops and the Conference of Major Religious Superiors, Dublin, 1993, Sections 15-17, p.5. Note also the detailed treatment of this theme in *The Religious Dimension of Education in a Catholic School,* Congregation for Catholic Education, London : Catholic Truth Society 1988, pp33-35.
19. See David Alvey, *Irish Education: The Case for Secular Reform,* Dublin : Athol Books, 1991, "The Case for Democracy," pp.94-101.
20. See Eoin G. Cassidy, "Irish Education: Examining the case for secular reform," *Studies,* Vol.81, Summer 1992, pp217-221.
21. Paul Andrews S.J., "Pluralism Revisited" in *Studies,* Vol.83, Summer 1994, p.153.
22. See the submission from Church of Ireland Board of Education *Response to the Green Paper on Education, 1992,* Dublin, 1992, esp. pp1-4, and that from the Catholic Archbishop of Dublin Dr. Desmond Connell, *Education for a Changing World,* Dublin, 1993, esp., pp3-4.
23. See Aine Hyland, "Educating Ireland's Children Together — the Dream and the Realities," address delivered at a seminar on the Green Paper in Kilkenny, 4th March 1993, Educate Together, 1993.
24. See the publication from the CMRS Education Commission, *Considered Response to the Green Paper,* Dublin, 1993, esp. pp5-15, and the article by the Irish theologian Dermot A. Lane, "Education and the Enterprise Culture," *Doctrine and Life,* October 1993, pp495-501.
25. For a detailed and finely balanced treatment of the legislative implications of our obligations as a signatory to international conventions/treaties, see *A Submission on the Green Paper on Education in terms of Human Rights, Justice, Equity and Peace,* The Irish Commission for Justice and Peace, Dublin, 1993. Included in this document is a compilation of the relevant extracts from international Human Rights documents related to education and a listing of all the International Human Rights instruments bearing on education. The submission to the NEC from the Department of Education, *Presentation to the National Education Convention,* Dublin, 1993, esp. pp10-11 shows evidence of a sensitivity to the importance of this issue.

26. See *Education for a Changing World,* pp31-32, 90-91, 96. In the *Report on the NEC* this issue merited a whole section entitled "Legal Aspects". See the report: The *Report on the NEC,* Section 16, pp131-132. It also featured prominently in the submission to the NEC from the Department of Education. See *Presentation to the National Education Convention,* Dublin, 1993, pp7-9.
27. Some of the more valuable attempts to unravel the complexities of this issue are to be found in a number of recently published articles, two by the law lecturer Michael J. Farry, "The Green Paper, the Church and the Constitution", *Studies,* Vol.82, Summer 1993, and "Education and the Constitution", *Studies,* Vol.83, Summer 1994, and one by the law lecturer Gerry Whyte, "Education and the Constitution," *Religion, Education and the Constitution,* ed. D. Lane, Dublin : Columba Press, 1992, pp84-117.
28. See the following passage from the section in the *Report on the NEC* entitled "Philosophy of Education and Policy Formation," "In successive contributions to the Convention there was a new awareness of the legitimate plurality of educational purposes and evidence of a mature commitment to the achievement of balance in educational aims" pp7-8.
29. *Education for a Changing World,* p.34.
30. See "The Declaration on Religious Liberty", Vatican 11: The Conciliar and Post Conciliar Documents, edited by Austin Flannery,O.P. (New York: Costello Publishing Company 1975), p.799-813.
31. (London: Catholic Truth Society 1988).
32. *Education for a Changing World,* p.217.
33. The *Report on the NEC,* p.8. See also the following passage taken from the "Background Paper" to the *Report on the NEC,* "The opportunity is now there to re-shape it (Irish Education) for the future, preserving what is valuable in the spiritual and cultural heritage while preparing the education system to respond to new needs and demands." The *Report on the NEC,* p.144.
34. In *Education for a Changing World,* Section 4:7 under the heading "The Role of Schools in Promoting Health and Well-Being" there is one passing reference to spiritual values which reads," The achievement of these objectives (providing

experiences which build the students self-esteem etc.) for all students will be influenced by ... as well as by the wider educational and spiritual values transmitted by the school," p.129.
35. In the *British Journal of Educational Studies*, Vol.xxxvii, May 1989, pp169-182. See also the article by Robin Minney, "What is Spirituality in an Educational context?" *British Journal of Educational Studies*, Vol.xxxix, November 1991, pp386-397.
36. *An Office For Standards in Education : discussion document*, London : OFSTED Publications Centre 1994.
37. ibid. p.8.
38. *Response to The NCCA consultative document on The Senior Cycle, 1990*, The Episcopal Working Committee on Developments in Education, Dublin, 1991, p.3. See also *The Religious Dimension of Education in a Catholic School*, Sections 52 and 60-61.
39. *Response to The NCCA consultative document on The Senior Cycle, 1990*, The Episcopal Working Committee on Developments in Education, Dublin, 1991, pp4-5. For a detailed treatment of this theme see The Religious Dimension of Catholic Education, Section 52-61.
40. For a succinct statement of the problems facing those concerned with promoting values education in the contemporary 'developed' world, See Philip Hughes and Malcolm Skilbeck, "Curriculum Reform ... Recent Trends and Issues," *The Curriculum Redefined: Schooling for the 21st Century*, OECD Documents, Paris : OECD 1994, p.22.
41. The Church of England Archbishop of York Dr. John Habgood argues convincingly for the importance of religion on this basis in an article entitled "Are Moral Values Enough?" *British Journal of Educational Studies*, Vol.xxxviii, May 1990, pp106-115. See also Kevin Williams, "Religious Ethos and State Schools, Doctrine and Life," Vol.42. November 1992. The contemporary philosopher Alasdair McIntyre is the classical exponent of the viewpoint that values which are not rooted in tradition will not survive in the contemporary culture of Liberalism. As a result of the cogency of his argumentation this viewpoint has, in recent years, achieved an increasing measure of acceptance.

42. The acknowledgement of this dimension of religious education in the submission to the NEC from Mary Immaculate College, Limerick, 1992, p.1.
43. *Response to Issues and Structures in Education, Academic Staff,* Mater Dei Institute, Dublin, 1984, pp3-4.
44. *Education for a Changing World,* pp.33-34.
45. See Aine Hyland, "Educating Ireland's Children Together — the Dream and the Realities," Address delivered at a seminar on the Green Paper in Kilkenny, 4th March 1993, Educate Together, 1993)
46. The *Report on the NEC,* Section 5 "Provision of Multi-Denomination and Secular Education," pp31-33.
47. Note the following statement from the Catholic Archbishop of Dublin Dr. Desmond Connell in the course of his submission to the NEC, "It is the Catholic case that the difference between the Catholic view and the secularist view of education is a fundamental, valid and relevant difference. It prevails over all other differences in education and consideration of this difference should be over-riding."(p.4)
48. *Education for a Changing World,* p.87, and The *Report on the NEC,* p.172.

NOTES

Dr. Joseph Dunne's Paper

1. *Report on the National Education Convention,* Dublin : National Education Convention Secretariat, 1994, p.7.
2. *Investment in Education,* Dublin : Stationery Office, 1965.
3. Ireland, *Education for a Changing World,* Green Paper, Dublin : Stationery Office, 1992, pp174-178.
4. See e.g. C. Whelan and B. Whelan, *Social Mobility in the Republic of Ireland : A Comparative Perspective,* Dublin : E.S.R.I., 1984; P. Clancy, *Who Goes to College,* A Second National Survey, Dublin : Higher Education Authority, 1988; and C.M.R.S., *Education and Poverty : Eliminating Disadvantage in the Primary School Years,* Dublin : CORI Education Commission, 1992.
5. The quotations here are from an exceptionally acute essay, D. O'Sullivan's "The Ideational Base of Irish Educational Policy," in D. Mulcahy and D. O'Sullivan, eds., *Irish Educational Policy : Process and Substance,* Dublin : Institute of Public Administration, 1989, pp264-245.
6. A rejection of just this kind of mysticism seems to be essential to the "affirmation of ordinary life," which Charles Taylor claims to be one of the defining characteristics of modernity, in *Sources of the Self : The Making of the Modern Identity,* Cambridge : Cambridge University Press, 1989.
7. Perhaps the most seminal elaboration in recent philosophy of the concept of a "practice" — to which my discussion here is much indebted — is in Alasdair MacIntyre's *After Virtue,* London : Duckworth, 1981, especially Chapter 14. See also W. Carr, "What is an Educational Practice?" *Journal of Philosophy of Education,* 24, 1990, pp15-24.

8. This point is developed a little in a later section,"Teaching and Learning in the light of Practices." Examples worth noting here of approaches to the teaching of the three activities mentioned are Donald Grave's approach to writing, various approaches to "paired reading" or "shared reading," and the Suzuki approach to musical performance. See D. Graves, *Writing : Teachers and Children at Work,* London : Heinemann, 1983; K.J. Topping and G.A. Lindsay, "Paired Reading : A Review of the Literature" in *Reading Papers in Education,* 7 (3), 1992, pp1-50, and S. Suzuki, *Nurtured by Love : A New Approach to Education,* New York : Exposition Press, 1969.

9. I refer here to the Greek concept of "praxis," and more particularly Aristotle's analysis of it. See J. Dunne, *Back to the Rough Ground : Phronesis and Techné in Modern Philosophy and in Aristotle,* Notre Dame and London : University of Notre Dame Press, 1993.

10. On this point, see R.K. Elliot, "Education, love of one's subject, and the love of truth," *Proceedings of the Philosophy of Education Society of Great Britain,* 8, 1, 1975, pp135-153; and Paddy Walsh, *Education and Meaning,* London : Cassell, 1993, p.164 ff.

11. *Education for a Changing World,* Green Paper, Dublin : Stationery Office, 1992, p.85.

12. The limitations of the technicist approach, and in particular the significance of the distinction between "Technique" and "Practice," is the major theme in Dunne, *op.cit.*

13. For a much fuller and more nuanced articulation of this point, see G. Gaden, *On the Participant's Engagement with his Activity and the Value of Specialisation in Post-Primary Education,* N.U.I., Ph.D. dissertation, 1985.

14. The latter responsiveness, which is at the heart of educative teaching, is well elucidated by Martin Buber under the rubric of "inclusion" in his essay, "Education," in *Between Man and Man,* London : Fontana, 1969.

15. R.G. Tarp and R. Gallimore, *Rousing Minds to Life,* Cambridge : Cambridge University Press, 1988, p.111.

16. See H. Gardner, *The Unschooled Mind : How Children Think and How Schools Should Teach,* London : Fontana, 1993.

17. The distinction I make here between two kinds of knowledge, and the importance as well as the difficulty of respecting both of them while bridging the gap between them, is a significant theme in writings in educational psychology and in philosophy. In educational psychology, see e.g. L. Vygotsky on the distinctions and relations between "scientific" concepts and "everyday" concepts in *Thinking and Speech,* Collected Works, Vol.1, New York : Plenum, 1987; Margaret Donaldson's similar points on "disembedded" knowledge and knowledge "supported by human sense" in *Children's Minds,* London : Fontana, 1978, especially Chapter 7, and H. Gardner's outline of evidence on the widespread inability of students in the United States to deploy specific domains of "school" knowledge in informal contexts when its relevance is not explicitly signalled to them, op.cit., Chapters.8 and 9. In philosophy and sociology, the "life-world" is an important concept for phenomenologists such as E.Husserl and A. Schutz; and recently the need for the enlightenment of the life-world by more formal "discursive" knowledge — as well as the danger of its being "colonised" by the latter — is a major theme in J. Habermas, *The Theory of Communicative Action,* 2 Vols., Boston : Beacon Press, 1984 and 1987. A closely related issue concerns the mediation between the "theoretical context of dialogue" and the "real" context of people's life-experience in P. Freire's attempt to construct a pedagogy that is both faithful to experience and facilitative of transformative insight, *Pedagogy of the Oppressed,* Harmondsworth : Penguin, 1972.
18. For recent writing on this point by influential authors, see A. Hargreaves, *Changing Teachers, Changing Times,* London : Cassell, 1994, and M. Fullan, *Changing Forces : Probing the Depths of Educational Reform,* Lewes : Falmer Press, 1993.
19. Without imputing responsibility to them for any of the views expressed here, I want to acknowledge the helpfulness to me in preparing this paper of conversations with Peter Archer, John Doyle, Gerry Gaden, Tom Kellaghan, Frank Litton and Father Fergal O'Connor, O.P.

NOTES

Dr. Kevin Williams' Paper

1. W. Shakespeare, *Hamlet,* Act 1, Sc. v. line 166.
2. Niamh Bhreathnach, Minister for Education, John Marcus O'Sullivan Lecture, "Towards a Coherent Philosophy of Education," *Irish Education Decision Maker,* 8, Spring, 1994, pp4-10, p.5.
3. This text of this debate can be found in John Hick, ed, *The Existence of God,* New York: The Macmillan Co., 1964, pp167-190. There is a very interesting exploration of this theme to be found in P. J. Hill, "Philosophical Disagreements and Self-Awareness," *Philosophical Studies,* 21, pp7-30.
4. This theme is explored in some detail in K. Williams, "Religious Ethos and State Schools," *Doctrine and Life,* 42, November, 1992, pp561-570.
5. On this issue see K. Williams, "Promoting the 'New Europe': Education or Proselytism?" *Studies,* (forthcoming, 1995) and "European Identity," *Doctrine and Life,* 44, January, 1994, pp19-25.
6. This metaphor was suggested to me by Signe Sandsmark.
7. K. Williams, "Church, State and Education," *Link Up,* 63, Feb. 1994, pp18-23.
8. *Essay Concerning Human Understanding,* London: Fontana/Collins, 1964, p.58.
9. Ibid., p.59.
10. In K. Williams, "Philosophy in the Classroom: A Word of Caution," *Rostrum,* Autumn, 1985, pp83-88, I give several examples of how philosophy can help us to detect nonsense and generally to reason more logically.
11. Paddy Walsh, *Education and Meaning: Philosophy in Practice,* London: Cassells, 1993; Donal Mulcahy, *Curriculum and Policy in Irish Post-Primary Education,* Dublin: Institute of Public Administration, 1981; Eamonn Callan, *Autonomy and Schooling,* Kingston and Montreal, McGill-Queen's University Press, 1988;

Daniel Murphy, *Martin Buber's Philosophy of Education*, Dublin: Irish Academic Press, 198; and *Tolstoy and Education*, Dublin: Irish Academic Press, 1992; Joseph Dunne, *Back to the Rough Ground: Phronesis and Techné in Modern Philosophy and in Aristotle*, (Indiana: Notre Dame University Press, 1993.

12. These categories are not to be conceived as mutually exclusive. Religion, for example, is a traditional subject where the element of personal education is particularly prominent. The multi-faceted character of religious education is considered in K. Williams, "The Necessary Angel: The Poetic Element in Religious Education", *The Furrow*, 40, September, 1989, pp537-541. The tension between these two aspects of religious education is addressed in A. G. McGrady and K. Williams, "Religious Education in the Republic of Ireland", Panorama (forthcoming, 1995).

13. This is confirmed by evidence from a survey conducted by Wilton Research and Marketing Ltd on behalf of *The Irish Independent* and published in that newspaper on December 13, 1993. The findings suggest an unease among the general population about the compulsory status of Irish. 68% of those surveyed felt that Irish should not be compulsory for the Leaving Certificate and a disturbingly high 65% felt that it should not even be compulsory for the Junior Certificate. 31% of those pupils questioned thought that Irish should be compulsory at Junior Certificate level and 24% thought that it should be compulsory for Leaving Certificate students. There is at least at a strong likelihood that many, if not, most of the 59% who thought that it should not be compulsory at Junior Certificate level and of the 65% who thought that it should not be compulsory at senior cycle would not choose to study the language if given a choice. An analysis of this survey, in the context of research reported in P. O'Riagáin and M. O'Gliasáin, *National Survey on Languages 1993: Preliminary Report*, Dublin : Institiúid Teangeolaíochta Eireann, 1994 can be found in K. Williams, "Why We should Stop Forcing the Language," *The Irish Independent*, 29 April 1994. On the issues of compulsion and choice in education and of compulsory Irish, in particular, see K. Williams, "Review Article: In Defence of Compulsory Education," *Journal of Philosophy of Education*, 24, 1990, pp285-294; "The Limits of Paternalism in Educational

Relations," *Irish Educational Studies,* 10, 1991, pp110-121; "Reason and Rhetoric in Curriculum Policy: An Appraisal of the Case for the Inclusion of Irish in the School Curriculum," *Studies,* 78, Summer 1989, pp191- 203.
14. See John Wilson, *Philosophy and Practical Education,* London, Boston and Henley : Routledge and Kegan Paul, 1977.
15. This phrase is taken from Wordsworth's poem, "The World is Too Much With Us," *Oxford Anthology of English Literature: Romantic Poetry and Prose,* Oxford : Oxford University Press, 1973.
16. This is why Margaret Donaldson describes abstract thought as "disembedded." See Chapter 7 of her book *Children's Minds,* London : Fontana Press, 1978, pp77-85.
17. W. Shakespeare, *Othello,* Act 1, Sc. i, lines 24-26.
18. See W. Shakespeare, *As You Like It,* Act II, Sc, vii, line 139. Consider also the lines from *Romeo and Juliet,* Act II, Sc. ii, lines 156/7. "Love goes towards love, as school boys from their books;/But love from love, toward school with heavy looks." The following is a quotation from Saint Jerome. If we spend more than an hour in reading, you will find us yawning and trying to restrain our boredom by rubbing our eyes; then as though we had been hard at work, we plunge once more into worldly affairs. I say nothing of the heavy meals which crush such mental faculties as we possess. I am ashamed to speak of our numerous calls, going ourselves every day to other people's houses, or waiting for others to come to us. Quoted in John Romer, *Testament: The Bible and History,* London : Michael O'Meara Books Ltd., 1988), p. 241.
19. John Kleinig, *Philosophical Issues in Education,* London and Sydney : Croom Helm, 1982, pp13, 17, 32-41 and R. Barrow and G. Milburn, *A Critical Dictionary of Educational Concepts: An Appraisal of Selected Ideas and Issues in Educational Theory and Practice,* New York and London: Harvester Wheatsheaf, 1990, p.249. See, above all, David Carr's, "Education, Learning and Understanding : The Process and the Product," *Journal of Philosophy of Education,* 26, 1992, pp215-225. Written in a sober, rigorous and invigorating idiom which would have commended itself to John Locke, this essay is a tour de force in contemporary philosophy of education.

20. For an account of these reservations regarding the plausibility of the distinction see K Williams, "The Classical Idiom in Curriculum Design," *Curriculum*, 11, 1990, pp132-140.
21. See Gilbert Ryle, *The Concept of Mind*, London : Hutchinson,1949, p. 31.
22. Ryle, *The Concept of Mind*, pp149-153, pp26-60.
23. These metaphors are taken from Michael Oakeshott. For details see Kevin Williams, "The Gift of an Interval: Michael Oakeshott's Idea of a University Education," *British Journal of Educational Studies*, 37, 1989, pp384-397.
24. Kleinig, *Philosophical Issues in Education*, p. 180.
25. See George F. Madaus and John Macnamara, *Public Examinations : A Study of the Irish Leaving Certificate*, Dublin : Educational Research Centre, St. Patrick's College, 1970, and also by the same authors, "The Quality of the Irish Leaving Certificate Examination," *The Irish Journal of Education*, 4, Summer 1970, pp5-18. For a discussion of this work, see Mulcahy, *Curriculum and Policy in Irish Post-Primary Education*, pp155-162.
26. See K. Williams, "Tradition and Fashion in Curriculum Design," *Oideas*, 31, Fomhar,1987, pp66-76. The locus classicus for discussion of this issue is, of course, Mulcahy, *Curriculum and Policy in Irish Post-Primary Education*.
27. I consider this matter in some detail in K. Williams, *Assessment : A Discussion Paper*, Dublin : ASTI, 1992, Chapter four. See also J. Boland and G. McNamara, "The Reform of Senior Cycle Educational Provision in the Republic of Ireland," *Irish Educational Studies*, 13, 1994, pp180-195.
28. Department of Education, *Leaving Certificate: Vocational Programme*, Dublin : The Stationery Office, n.d.
29. Based on the statistics provided in National Council for Curriculum and Assessment, *The 1991 Leaving Certificate Examination : A Review of Results*, Dublin : The Stationery Office, 1992.
30. See Margaret Donaldson, *Children's Minds*, p. 84.
31. Theodore Lewis, "Difficulties Attending the New Vocationalism in the USA," *Journal of Philosophy of Education*, 25, 1991, pp95-108, pp104, 96.
32. See Gilbert Ryle, "Ordinary Language" in Collected Papers, Vol. 2, London : Hutchinson, 1971, p. 306.

33. See G. Ryle, "Knowing How and Knowing That" in *Collected Papers*, Vol. 2.
34. D. F. Hannan and S. Shortall, *The Quality of Their Education: School Leavers' Views of Educational Objectives and Outcomes*, Paper 153, Dublin : The Economic and Social Research Institute, 1991.
35. Association of Secondary Teachers, Ireland, *Staffing, Funding and Facilities in Second Level Schools*, Dublin: Association of Secondary Teachers, Ireland, 1991, p. 9; T. Crooks, T. and J. McKernan, *The Challenge of Change: Curriculum Development in Irish Post-Primary Schools 1970-1984*, Dublin : Institute of Public Administration, 1984, p. 119.
36. Ibid. This section of the essay touches on issues explored in detail in K. Williams, "Vocationalism and Liberal Education," Journal of Philosophy of Education, 28, 1994, pp89-100.
37. This view is shared by employers. For example, in a survey of 150 companies, employers were invited to rate skills and personal qualities in order of importance. 70% of the respondents rated oral communications, 58% written communications, 48% numeracy, 46%, enterprise/initiative, 39%, problem solving, 26%, foreign language skills, 22% creativity, 18%, computer systems, 15%, keyboard skills. See Confederation of Irish Industry, "Human resources — The Key Issues", *CII Newsletter*, Vol. 53. No. 9, 1990, pp1-7.
38. Ibid. 21% of employers rate numeracy skills as excellent or very good, 19% give this rating to oral communications, 12% to enterprise and initiative, 10% to written communications and 3% to languages.
39. These are covered in some detail in my first book, *The Vocational Preparation Course : An Educational Appraisal and Practical Guide*, Dublin : Association of Secondary Teachers, Ireland, 1985, which is now, alas, out of print and available only in libraries.
40. Reference to this incident first appeared in Williams, "Vocationalism and Liberal Education."
41. For references see ibid, p. 99.
42. I am grateful to Fiona Williams, Helen Walsh, Kevin Shortall, and Erica Sheehan for their comments on this article.

NOTES

Dr. Pádraig Hogan's Paper

1. Thomas Aquinas *Summa Theologiae,* Translated by the English Dominican Fathers, London : Blackfriars, in association with Eyre and Spottiswoode, 1963-1974.
2. Friedrich Nietzsche *Beyond Good and Evil: Prelude to a Philosophy of the Future* (1886), Translated by R.J. Hollingdale, with Introduction by Michael Tanner, London : Penguin, 1973, 1990, §259.
3. Friedrich Nietzsche, *On the Genealogy of Morals* (1887), Translated by Walter Kaufmann and R. J. Hollingdale, New York : Vintage Press, 1968, III, 28.
4. *Beyond Good and Evil,* §62; *On the Genealogy of Morals,* III, 14,15.
5. *On the Genealogy of Morals,* III, 11.
6. *On the Genealogy of Morals,* III, 14; *Beyond Good and Evil,* §188.
7. *Beyond Good and Evil,* p. 6.
8. Friedrich Nietzsche, *Thus Spoke Zarathustra* (1883-85), Translated with an Introduction by R.J. Hollingdale, London : Penguin, 1961, 1986, Prologue, 3 ff; II, 12, 13.
9. *Ibid,* I, 10, 11.
10. These three designations are associated respectively with Aristotelian philosophy, Classical economics, and Cartesian epistemology.
11. Plato, *Apology,* 23.

A Note on the Speakers

Mr. Barney O'Reilly, M.Ed. is Chief Executive Officer of Tralee VEC. He has made many contributions to educational debate in recent years and has been active also in advancing the quality of that debate — through participating in conferences on educational management and administration, through organising events such as the annual John Marcus O' Sullivan Memorial Lecture and its related seminars, and also as joint editor of Irish Education — *Decision Maker*. Among his writings which are pertinent to the theme of the symposium is the article "Sub-National Structures for Irish Education," in *Decision Maker*, No.5, Spring 1992.

Dr. Eoin Cassidy is a priest of the Archdiocese of Dublin. He is Head of the Philosophy Department at Mater Dei Institute and also lectures in philosophy in Holy Cross College Clonliffe. In recent years he has been a visiting lecturer in philosophy in Queen's University Belfast and in Kachebere College, Malawi. Among his recent publications is an article related to the theme of the current symposium entitled: "Irish Educational Policy in a Philosophical Perspective— The Legacy of Liberalism," in *Religion, Education and the Constitution*, edited by Dermot Lane (Dublin: Columba Press, 1992).

Dr. Joseph Dunne is a lecturer in Philosophy of Education at St. Patrick's College, Drumcondra. He has published many scholarly articles and reviews and is author of a recently published major work on classical and modern philosophy: *Back to the Rough Ground — Phronesis and Techne in Modern Philosophy and in Aristotle* (Notre Dame & London : University of Notre Dame Press, 1993). Among his articles which are pertinent to the theme of the symposium is "The Catholic School and Civil Society: Exploring the Tensions," in *The Catholic School in Contemporary Society* (Dublin, Conference of Major Religious Superiors, 1991).

Dr. Kevin Williams is a lecturer in Education at the Mater Dei Institute, Dublin. He has published widely on educational and philosophical issues in Irish and international journals. He is author of the book *Assessment — A Discussion Paper* (Dublin : ASTI 1992). Another of his recent writings which is pertinent to the theme of the symposium is "Vocationalism and Liberal Education," in *Journal of Philosophy of Education,* Vol. 28, No.1, 1994 (Oxford : Carfax). He is currently Vice-President of the Educational Studies Association of Ireland.

Dr. Pádraig Hogan is a lecturer in Education at St. Patrick's College, Maynooth, and has spoken and published frequently on educational issues in Ireland and abroad. Among his writings which are pertinent to the symposium are "The Sovereignty of Learning, the Fortunes of Schooling and the New Educational Virtuousness," in *British Journal of Educational Studies,* Vol. 40, No.2, 1992 (Oxford : Blackwell) and "The Practice of Education and the Courtship of Youthful Sensibility", in *Journal of Philosophy of Education,* Vol 27, No.1, 1993 (Oxford: Carfax). He was General Editor of the journal *Irish Educational Studies* from 1990-94 and is currently President of the Educational Studies Association of Ireland.